Modern Critical Views

Modern Critical Views

JOHN IRVING

Edited and with an introduction by
Harold Bloom
Sterling Professor of the Humanities
Yale University

CHELSEA HOUSE PUBLISHERS
Philadelphia

© 2001 by Chelsea House Publishers, a subsidiary of
Haights Cross Communications.

Introduction © 2001 by Harold Bloom.

Printed and bound in the United States of America

10 9 8 7 6 5 4 3 2 1

∞ The paper used in this publication meets the minimum
requirements of the American National Standard for
Permanence of Paper for Printed Library Materials,
Z39.48-1984

Library of Congress Cataloging-in-Publication Data

John Irving / edited and with an introduction by Harold Bloom.
        p.   cm.
        Includes bibliographical references and index.
        ISBN 0-7910-5920-0 (alk. paper)
        1. Irving, John, 1942–   —Criticism and interpretation.
    I. Bloom, Harold.   II. Series.

    PS3559.R8 Z72 2001
    813'.54—dc21   00-060229
                                                CIP

Chelsea House Publishers
1974 Sproul Road, Suite 400
Broomall, PA 19008-0914

The Chelsea House World Wide Web address is
http://www.chelseahouse.com

Contributing Editor: Erica da Costa

Produced by: Robert Gerson Publisher's Services, Santa Barbara, CA

Contents

Editor's Note

My Introduction centers upon *The World According to Garp*, which I judge to be a period piece.

Greil Marcus begins the chronological sequence of critical essays with an appreciation of *Garp's* exuberance, while Benjamin DeMott judges *The Hotel New Hampshire* to be comparable to Salinger, Vonnegut, and the Beatles, rather than to Irving's prime precursor, Scott Fitzgerald.

In an overview, Michael Priestly explores Irving's struggles with narrative perspective, after which Robert Towers finds *The Hotel New Hampshire* to be a lesser work than *Garp*.

Joseph Epstein explains Irving's popularity as this novelist's ability "to make his readers feel advanced in their views yet fundamentally sound in their emotions," while Gabriel Miller finds *The 158-Pound Marriage* to be derivative but interestingly enigmatic.

A defense of Irving is made by Jane Bowers Hill, for whom Irving, like Vonnegut, is a popular writer who seeks to transcend rules and limitations. This is akin to Raymond J. Wilson III, who finds in *Garp* a successful instance of Post-Modernism.

Debra Shostak traces in Irving the family romance of influence-anxiety, after which Philip Page examines the parodistic complexities of *A Prayer for Owen Meany*.

In this book's final essay, Todd F. Davis and Kenneth Womack praise *The Cider House Rules* as a successful instance of a modern Dickensian novel.

Introduction

John Irving's popularity began with his fourth published novel, *The World According to Garp* (1978). His two other large successes have been *The Hotel New Hampshire* (1981) and *The Cider House Rules* (1985). *A Prayer for Owen Meany* (1989) did not attract Irving's full audience, yet seems to me his most ambitious work, though deeply haunted by his unsettled relationship to literary tradition. The 1990s saw some diminishment in Irving's formidable energies, and he seemed, at decade's end, to be more interested in movie-making than in fresh attempts at narrative fiction.

Rereading *The World According to Garp* twenty years later is a mixed experience, since the novel itself is a rather eclectic mix. It starts out as a Joycean portrait of the artist as a young man, but turns into a Pynchonian "Postmodernist" parody. As story, it has a singular exuberance, and remains readable, though essentially it is a period piece, as all of Irving's novels and stories seem fated to become.

Broadly, there are two sorts of "popular novelists." The Grisham-King-Clancy-Crichton variety are not particularly "literary." John Irving, like Tom Wolfe, has serious aesthetic aspirations. Wolfe attempts to invoke Balzac and Zola, while Irving wants to enter the sphere of Dickens. Yet Wolfe remains an involuntary imitator of Hemingway, while Irving cannot cut loose from Scott Fitzgerald's prose style.

What then survives of *The World According to Garp*? Literary echoes (as opposed to controlled allusions) are everywhere: Joyce, John Updike, John Barth, Fitzgerald, Pynchon, and more, many more. And many literary genres are mixed together: farce, fantasy, the Gothic, the saga of personal development, "metafiction," almost what-you-will. Though the mix is generally readable, the implausible is always with us.

In Dickens, the implausible almost always is made plausible by the storyteller's art. Irving desires that uncanny transformation, yet cannot achieve it. Dickens of course is too huge a paradigm, so it is more useful to contrast Irving to the late Iris Murdoch, who closely followed Dickens in exploiting coincidence and in risking the grotesque. Where Murdoch frequently makes her audacities work, Irving rarely does.

The World According to Garp fails to shape itself, whether as novel or as world. Whether it even shapes itself as prose is disputable; here is the novel's conclusion:

> In the world according to her father, Jenny Garp knew, we must have energy. Her famous grandmother, Jenny Fields, once thought of us as Externals, Vital Organs, Absentees, and Goners. But in the world according to Garp, we are all terminal cases.

"Terminal cases," in so large a context, is misplaced wit, at best. We have an interval, as Walter Pater wrote, and then our place knows us no more. Pater achieves the memorable; the fictive Garp cannot.

GREIL MARCUS

Garp: Death in the Family

John Irving's *The World According to Garp* must be one of the few good American novels in which more characters are killed off than in Dashiell Hammett's *Red Harvest*. But *Red Harvest*, after all, is about a gang war. *The World According to Garp* is set within the matrix of family life: it turns around a mother and her son, a father and his daughter, husbands, wives and children.

I've never been able to keep track of all the deaths in *Red Harvest*—I tend to lose count after the chapter entitled "The Seventeenth Murder"—but I felt the need to make a list for *Garp*. Including the characters in the books and tales of T.S. Garp himself, who is a novelist when he is not a cook, househusband or wrestling coach—and these characters should be included, because their presence is usually as full-bodied, and their extinction as compelling, as that of the "real" characters in *Garp*—the body count comes to something over fifty. (I was unsure whether to mark down the bear that dies of diarrhea, or the sheep and calf a farm boy kills after he fucks them.) Some notes from my ledger:

Dies in war. Dies of apoplexy after snowball fight. Freezes to death. Plane crash (two). Beggar murdered by drowning. Anarchist eaten by zoo animals. Chokes to death on chewing gum. Chokes to death on olive. Throat cut. Drowns. Falls out of plane (two). Strangles when tie is caught in escalator. Killed in car crash. Dies in car crash after attempted murder. Shot. Shot. Shot.

From *Rolling Stone* (24 August 1978 and 21 September 1978). © 1978 by Greil Marcus.

Which is not to mention various rapes and maimings, including castration as the accidental result of oral sex.

Few of the men and women in *Garp* who die of "natural causes" get to do so in bed; for that matter, in *Garp* "natural causes" almost always means cancer or heart attack, the two diseases that today carry the heaviest connotations of violence and guilt. And almost everyone dies, as the phrase goes, prematurely. Just before the Reaper comes for Helen Holm, Garp's wife, the omniscient narrator informs us that Helen "lived a long, long time"; one may be taken aback to find that this approbation, rare as rocs' eggs in *Garp*, is granted to one who dies well short of her sixtieth birthday—probably close to twenty years short of what the insurance companies tell us is the average life span of a middle-class white woman like Helen Holm.

Irving has written a book full of grotesque, perverse, sensational incidents—the action in *The World According to Garp* is parodied, but also extended, in *The World According to Bensenhaver*, the novel Garp writes after the accident in which Helen's lover loses his penis, Garp's and Helen's youngest son loses his life, and their oldest son loses his right eye—but the book cannot really be described by any of those words. People are dying almost from the first page, but by the end the reader is neither bored with death nor hardened to it. Instead, an awful, beautiful aura of appropriateness settles over the novel. It's a strange, *Moby Dick*-like sense of completeness. One accepts what happens to Irving's characters, even though what happens may make one squirm, protest, or feel real grief. One accepts it because one has come to accept Irving's characters: as people, as friends, even though they too may be grotesque, perverse or sensational.

Irving blurs the line we tend to draw between "ordinary" and violent death, just as he erases the line that in fiction conventionally separates "normal" and perverse characters. In most novels we get one or the other, or we find the normal and the perverse in opposition, fighting over the definition of life. "The world according to Irving" might be a world in which the normal and the perverse coexist without ever considering that they shouldn't—or couldn't.

Take, for example, Irving's two most outrageous inventions, Roberta Muldoon and the Ellen Jamesians. Roberta Muldoon, best friend of Garp, of Jenny Fields (Garp's mother, a celibate nurse and accidental feminist heroine) and in later years of Helen Holm, is a transsexual. But not just any transsexual: she is the former Robert Muldoon, known all over America as Number Ninety, the vicious tight end for the Philadelphia Eagles. Such a setup gives Irving the opportunity for a lot of comedy, and he uses it: *Garp* is a comic novel suffused with menace and forgiveness. But when one has closed the book, it's clear that by taking the edge off his transsexual by making her transformation absurd—by pitching it on the most distant frontier of possibility—Irving makes us accept Roberta as anything but absurd.

Rejecting her genetic identity as a man, but never really rejecting her identity as the meanest body blocker in the NFL, Roberta comes to life as profoundly as any character in *Garp*, and the edge returns more sharply than ever, dulled neither by clichés nor cheap pathos. Like Jenny Fields, who takes Roberta under her wing in the hard days following her sex-change operation, Roberta becomes the rock the other characters in *Garp* can lean against: she seeks the role and lives up to it. The most affecting moment of the book—a shining, devastating moment—comes just after *her* death, as, at an Eagles-Cowboys game, Roberta's number is flashed on the scoreboard, and the crusty radio announcer, far out of his depth, searches desperately for a way to memorialize Roberta ("She had a great pair of hands," is his first, fumbling try), and, miraculously, succeeds. But even that scene does not match the grace of the words Jenny Garp, Garp's and Helen's daughter, finds to break the news of Roberta's death to her brother, who by this time has a missing arm to go with his missing eye. "Bad news, Duncan," Jenny Garp says. "Old Number Ninety has dropped the ball."

The Ellen Jamesians are the most disturbing and pathetic presence in the book. They are the adversaries of Garp, Helen and Roberta; the friends of Jenny Fields, who takes them in as she takes in all female strays who come to her.

After Garp and Helen marry, Jenny Fields, famous and much followed-around after the surprise success of her autobiography, *A Sexual Suspect*, arrives at Garp's apartment with a large, speechless companion. She explains the woman's silence:

"You haven't heard of Ellen James?" Jenny asked.

"No," Garp admitted.

"Well, there's a whole *society* of women now," Jenny informed him, "because of what happened to Ellen James."

"What happened to her?" Garp asked.

"Two men raped her when she was eleven years old," Jenny said. "Then they cut off her tongue so she couldn't tell anyone who they were or what they looked like. They were so stupid they didn't know an eleven-year-old could *write*. Ellen James wrote a very careful description of the men, and they were caught, and they were tried and convicted. In jail, someone murdered them."

"Wow," Garp said. "So *that's* Ellen James?" he whispered, indicating the big quiet woman with new respect.

Jenny rolled her eyes again. "No," she said. "That is someone from the Ellen James *Society.* Ellen James is still a child."

"You mean this Ellen James Society goes around not talking," Garp said, "as if they didn't have any tongues?"

"No, I mean they *don't* have any tongues," Jenny said. "People in the Ellen James Society have their tongues cut off. To protest what happened to Ellen James."

"Oh boy," Garp said, looking at the large woman with renewed dislike.

"They call themselves the Ellen Jamesians," Jenny said.

"I don't want to hear any more of this shit, Mom," Garp said.

Garp's attitude toward the Ellen Jamesians—the Furies of *The World According to Garp*, as it turns out—is easily summed up:

"I'll tell you something about these women, Mom," he said to Jenny once. "They were probably all lousy at talking anyway; they probably never had a worthwhile thing to say in their lives— so their tongues were no great sacrifice; in fact, it probably saves them considerable embarrassment. If you see what I mean."

"You're a little short on sympathy," Jenny told him.

"I have *lots* of sympathy—for Ellen James," Garp said.

"These women must have suffered, in other ways, themselves," Jenny said. "That's what makes them want to get closer to each other."

"And inflict more suffering on themselves, Mom?"

"Rape is every woman's problem," Jenny said.

"It's every man's problem, too, Mom. The next time there's a rape, suppose I cut my *prick* off and wear it around my neck. Would you respect *that*, too?"

"We're talking about *sincere* gestures," Jenny said.

"We're talking about *stupid* gestures," Garp said.

Eventually Ellen James herself comes into Garp's life, becomes a member of his family ("I am *not* an Ellen Jamesian," she scribbles to him as she and Garp meet: "I would never do [*that*] to myself"), and by this time, the Ellen Jamesians seem condemned, by Irving's novel as well as by Garp, as mere crazies, or perhaps as one novelist's attempt to stay ahead of the craziness of American life. But as it happens, Irving sneaks in a scene in which an Ellen Jamesian takes on an undeniable dignity. At Jenny Fields' funeral a speaker breaks down, and leaves the stage. The woman who has been at her side remains, in silence, to face down the huge crowd. "The big, tough-looking woman wanted to say something," Irving writes, "and the audience waited. But they would wait forever to hear a word from her." So the Ellen Jamesians, too, are given their claim on life. That means that none of the other characters in *Garp*, nor its readers, can escape them—and they have a lot more work to do before they finally fade away.

II

"It wasn't as if they were just characters in a novel," my mother said of her reaction to the deaths of the people who make their way through John Irving's *The World According to Garp*—people who are, of course, characters in a novel.

Garp is harder to take, and more exhilarating, than one has any right to expect. One friend told me that my first column on *Garp*, which began with a list of disasters and tragedies that occur in the novel would have put her off had she not already begun the book. "All that violence," she said. "If you give people the idea that's what the book *is*, who's going to want to read it?" And then, to drive home her point, that *Garp* is much richer, more subtle, than my emphasis on its violence suggested, she proceeded to describe her response to a long rape scene, perhaps the most horrific section of the book. "Little noises kept coming out of my throat," said my friend, who as it happens, has worked as a rape counselor for some years and has calmed rape victims whose stories were far worse than any Irving has to offer. "I couldn't stop the sounds. It was the best, the toughest rape scene I've ever read."

Clearly, my friend was talking about more than the "violence" of this particular sequence. Her response—her terror, empathy, and fury—had to do with the way Irving shows us what's going on inside the victim's mind; with the scared courage she draws on to save herself; with the brutal, utterly serious humor of the detective who breaks every rule of procedure to track the rapist down. Her response had to do with the fact that in *The World According to Garp* life is, more than anything else, intense . . . sharp-edged, and dangerous: the book is about the worst fears of its characters coming true.

But what, then, is going on in this book, if a focus on its violence is misleading—but that violence is still central, necessary to its power? The answer isn't to be found in T.S. Garp's (and Irving's) explicit credo, the last words of the book: "We are all terminal cases." Such words might be meant to seem inscrutably profound, in just the way the last shot of Chaplin's *City Lights* is; but reading them, or applying them back to make sense of what one's read, one doesn't feel that existence has been magically clarified, that one's very soul has been simultaneously lifted up to heaven and driven down to hell. Incidents in *Garp* may do that, but not the ideas that are brought forth to explain them. "We are all terminal cases" is a slipknot of an idea, a graceful statement of the obvious. It takes one no distance worth traveling.

Rather, violence and death in *Garp* hurt deeply because the lives Irving creates for his characters are full to bursting with humor, purpose, lust, revenge, love, eccentricity and the will to keep promises. The struggle defined in *Garp* is not the hopeless struggle of men and women to beat the Reaper (as "We are all terminal cases" seems to imply), but the struggle of certain men and women to keep faith with each other.

One becomes attuned to what is lost when these people die. One understands just how their deaths will leave gaps—bleeding holes—in the lives of those who, for the time being, survive them. Those I've talked to have actually mourned the people in this book, and the mourning is complex, bitter, confused, and sustaining. The reader's mourning is not unlike that of Irving's characters. And this is so because Irving has written what, these days anyway, is the rarest sort of novel: a long, unsentimental, intricate, unfaked story about people who are basically good.

Garp is about the necessity and the limits of morals, which are seen as essential to a decent life, but which, no matter if you attach yourself to a moral system or draw morals out of yourself, can take you only so far; evil is identified with amorality (not the refusal of morals, but their absolute absence) and represented by rapists, only one of whom is given more than the thinnest presence. Some of Irving's principal characters are stupid, some are crazy, but none are corrupt—and Irving does not make the easy mistake of equating evil with stupidity or insanity. Evil, to Irving, is a fact of life. Good is much more interesting, much harder to get a fix on, much harder to bring off.

In *Garp*'s terms, good might be identified with those who manage to live in their own worlds without refusing to live in those of others—without denigrating them. Jenny Fields decides to live on her own, which for her means without sex; still, she wants a child, and in order to get one, copulates (for the first and last time of her life) with a brain-damaged casualty of World War II, one of her charges in the hospital where she works. He conveniently expires; she goes on to become head nurse at a New England boarding school, where her son Garp is raised and educated. Garp decides, at an early age, to turn himself into a novelist; along the way, he becomes a wrestler. Much of his life is spent in finding his voice, and finding people to listen to it—and hear what he has to say. This includes "the public," but it also includes his wife, Helen Holm and his children: one of the book's strongest moments (and one of Garp's best pieces of fiction) comes when Garp tells his little son Walt an amazingly grisly tale about a cat run over by a car—a cautionary tale, really, since Garp's purpose is not only to practice his craft as one who makes things up, but to convince his son to be careful crossing the street. Helen Holm, raised by her father Ernie, Garp's wrestling coach (her mother has abandoned them), is an English professor; she lives her own, not sharply described life within the confines of her family, and far more than Garp takes those actions that determine the shape of their life together.

Each of these people is to some degree apart from the others, from all others: they love, they are devoted, but they are incapable of surrender to anyone else. The connections they make to others are deep, but on their own terms.

Their motives, when they act, have to do with a refusal to do the prudent thing and shrivel up inside, and with a refusal to block out the world and wall themselves off with egotism. Jenny Fields, after all, does not become a nun, or a hermit; Garp does not care only for his art; though Helen's relationship with her children is very shadowy, it's clear her family is a great deal more than a base of operations or a badge of respectability. Perhaps what makes Jenny, Garp and Helen good is that they recognize the tension between themselves and their family, and try to walk the line.

But to say that these people are good is not to say that they're benign, or that their struggle to keep faith with each other isn't marked—even shaped—by betrayals. Garp, young and happily married, knocks off one-night stands with baby sitters. Helen seems to accept this when she hears about it, but the knowledge never really settles; her resentment is at least partly at the root of a much more serious affair she initiates with a student years later—an affair that, in an astonishing tangle of fate, guilty knowledge, anger, fear, good will and common sense, leads straight to an accident that nearly destroys Garp's and Helen's family. In other words, to say that these people are good doesn't mean good is what they create. They are honest, and intense, and without ever accepting the havoc they may wreak as the price one pays for refusing certain compromises—and such an acceptance underlies most serious fiction today—they try to push that honesty and that intensity to the limit, and to take those they care about with them. It works, too: Garp inherits that spirit from his mother, and his children inherit it from him.

Jenny, Garp and Helen are wildly likable; each is very tough, very smart, and Garp and Helen share a wit that could drop an intruder at forty feet. They are loyal, nervy, never dull. In a different book, they would be too likable, too "good"—though not in the way Irving develops the concept. Now, given the nature of modern fiction, which has to countenance Freud and sixty years of organized mass murder to appear both convincing and true to its time, we tend to distrust the notion that people are, or even can be, good. We've learned to distrust a character's motives, not to share them—goodness is the domain of *Love Story* and *Jonathan Livingston Seagull*. Any book that tries to make good real runs the risk of sappiness—of Erich Segal's mindlessness or Kurt Vonnegut's woebegone banality.

But *Garp* is not sappy, and Garp's/Irving's "We are all terminal cases" to the contrary, it's neither woebegone nor banal. Irving deals with Freud—that is, with our suspicion of explicit motives—by writing as if, yes, motives are buried, mysterious, but no less real for all that: mystery is not a problem to be solved but an element of being. And he deals with mass murder—that is, with the political frame of reference of our lives—by personalizing and privatizing it. One of the most extraordinary things about *Garp* is that while most of the action is set during the time of the Vietnam War, the war is never mentioned, and yet is in the book anyway: the war is in the book the way the war was in *John Wesley Harding*, as a specter of uncertainty, fear, and death, as a specter to which one must respond by refusing to talk cheaply, or act casually. The lives of the characters in *Garp* are touched with violence not only because they produce it, but because violence is loose, appealing, pornographically exciting. As in a war, any act, any statement, can be lethal. But you can't look over your shoulder in every direction at once.

It is the violence in *Garp*, finally, that anchors the book. It anchors the action and the fate of the character to a reality outside their own, and it anchors the characters to their own reality. Given what Irving has in store for them, Garp, Helen and Jenny could be sappy only if they were able to shrug off disaster, to trivialize it, and nothing could be farther from what they actually do. Rather, they live as if no moment could possibly be trivial. All things are opportunities for humor, dread, and good will, and so they make the most of them.

BENJAMIN DeMOTT

Domesticated Madness

In 1960, the book of the year in academic literary circles was Leslie Fiedler's *Love and Death in the American Novel*. It claimed that our authors are obsessed with darkness and the grotesque, disinclined to represent adult heterosexual love or normal familial relationships, and bent on producing a literature that's fundamentally "nonrealist, sadist, and melodramatic." This was a sensible thesis, on the whole, but, not astonishingly, one can think of writers whose work doesn't support it. The last two novels by a bright new star on our fictional scene, for instance, announce a possibility that *Love and Death* fails to imagine, namely that of conjoining, in a single literary work, the grotesquely dark and the sunny and solid—everyday middle experience of the kind once described as "safe as houses."

The novelist in question is, of course, John Irving, author of the best-selling *The World According to Garp* and of *The Hotel New Hampshire*. Irving came to notice with a book strictly observant, as would have been remarked had the work won more readers, of several Fiedlerian specifications: *Setting Free the Bears* (1968) is about two young males larking around Mitteleuropa on motorbikes, loving and leaving girls, becoming increasingly involved with each other, and committing themselves to no project longer-termed than that of raiding the Hietzinger Zoo, in Vienna, for the purpose of releasing caged animals. Two other novels preceded *Garp*, neither breaking new

From *Atlantic Monthly* 248, no. 4 (October 1981). © 1981 by the Atlantic Monthly Company.

aesthetic ground. With *Garp* came revelation. That book's bravura array included several of the goriest scenes (a rapist carved to death in the act by his victim, for instance) yet contributed to our letters. But immediately adjacent to those scenes stood chapter upon chapter of domestic trivia—kitchen duty, kid-watching, and one wholly treasurable passage in which an anxious parent dares to observe, secretly, the performance of another parent to whom he has entrusted the care, overnight, of his young.

The Hotel New Hampshire builds on this unusual foundation. In essence it's a family chronicle—a tale of generations of parents coping with children and siblings coping with each other. The chief parents are Win and Mary Berry of Dairy, New Hampshire, a couple brought together after high school at a seaside resort where, on summer jobs, they catch a glimpse of a joyous vocation (innkeeping). The Berry union produces five spirited and amusing children: Lilly, who becomes a successful novelist (her subject is childhood); Frank, who becomes a literary agent; Franny, who grows up to marry a black pro football player; John, the book's narrator, whose passions include jogging and weight-lifting; and Egg, the youngest child, who's killed in an accident at the age of seven. The story covers a quarter-century, beginning round about 1940, and the principal action takes place in three hotels, each called— for insufficient cause, I think—The Hotel New Hampshire. (The hotels are situated in New Hampshire, Austria, and Maine.)

Family dailiness—traditional sitcom material—is in nearly constant view throughout the novel. Father and mother tell stories about their youth to their children. Grandfather teaches grandson his special athletic skills. Mother intercedes when older siblings try to force their juniors into premature knowingness. Mother speaks out against slovenliness. ("Your room, Lilly," Mother said. "What am I going to say about your room?") Children tease each other ferociously, engage in fist-fights, learn to work together in the family business, learn to drive cars, learn forbearance, find their affection for one another strengthening over time. And toward the end, children are seen taking up parental roles, caring for the elders whose hour as nurturers and protectors has begun to fade. Four of the eight family members with whom this book begins are gone at the end, but the survivors are close-knit, and a new Berry baby is on the way, assuring the continuity of the generations.

Simple, unsadistic stuff. But, as I've hinted, it's conjoined with matter remote from everyday, and the combination creates surprising narrative rhythms and a sharply distinctive tone. *The Hotel New Hampshire* is structured as a succession of shrewdly prepared explosions of violence, each of which blends the hideous and the comic, and projects a fresh length of story line that hisses forward into the next blowup almost before the dust of the last has settled. A typical sequence runs as follows: Franny Berry is gang-raped by members of a prep school football team on Hallowe'en; on the same day, her father, Win Berry, takes the family pet, an ancient Labrador named Sorrow who is dear to Franny but troublingly afflicted with flatulence, to the local vet to be put to sleep. Conscious of his fearfully violated younger sister's need for the comfort of her pet, Frank Berry races to the animal hospital in hope of saving the beast. He's too late, but he does recover Sorrow's body, and, having earlier learned taxidermy in a biology course, resolves to stuff the dog and offer it to his sister as a gift. New narrative fuse lit and burning, obviously, and explosion is imminent. It occurs a chapter later, on Christmas Day. Stuffed and mounted in an "attack" pose, hidden in an upstairs closet, Sorrow suddenly springs out at Grandfather Berry when the latter, working out with weights in his room, accidentally knocks open the closet door:

> . . . before I could get my breath back and tell my grandfather that it was only a Christmas present for Franny—that it was only one of Frank's awful projects from down at the bio lab—the old [man] slung his barbell at the savage attack dog and threw his wonderful lineman's body back against me (to protect me, no doubt; that must have been what he meant to do) . . . [and] dropped dead in my arms.

The rape-taxidermy sequence shuttles swiftly between the farcical and the pathetic. Franny Berry's anguished weeping is in our ears as we watch her brother push the stiffening dog's body into a trash bag (the vet's wife murmurs, "It's so sweet"). We jump cut from Franny's shattered effort to convince herself that her assailants haven't really damaged the "*me* in me" to a series of one-liners exchanged by brothers discussing dog-stuffing. (Brother John: "I don't know if Franny will like that." Brother Frank: "It's the next-best thing to being alive.") We're never in doubt of Frank Berry's sympathy for his sister's suffering, but the gags superimposed upon this sympathy do contort it. And comparable contortions abound elsewhere in the book's action. The primary moment of catharsis occurs when the Berry children, with aides, manage to terrify the rapists' ringleader with a brilliantly staged threat that he himself will be raped by a bear. The book's narrative crisis occurs when Father Berry handily smashes (with a Louisville Slugger) a ring of terrorists in the Austrian Hotel New Hampshire who are about to blow up Vienna's opera house and take the Berry family hostage. Always, the sympathy and solidarity of the family members are in evidence— qualities placing the Berrys firmly in a world of light and affirmation. But often the visible deeds and spoken words verge upon the violently sadistic, or the black comic, or the melodramatically grotesque.

And the author's taste for incongruity affects characterization as well as action. Each of the Berrys is normal in his or her feeling for parents and siblings—loving, concerned, loyal:

"... we *aren't* eccentric, we're *not* bizarre. To each other," Franny would say, "we're as common as rain." And she was right: to each other, we were as normal and nice as the smell of bread, we were just a family.

But it's a fact that the Berry kids don't invariably sound "normal and nice." On the first page of the book, one child speculates to another about the precise date when their parents "started screwing"; from then on the children's sprightly R-rated obscenities decorate virtually every paragraph. Nor can it be said that these folks are untouched by deviance. Franny Berry is, for an interval, caught in a lesbian love affair. She and John Berry are in love with each other and consummate their incestuous passion in an extended sexual bout. Frank Berry is an out-of-the-closet homosexual given to expressions of glee in his aberrancy. Lilly Berry is a suicide.

The entire family, furthermore, thrives on exposure to ills of the public world that more conventional families labor to avoid. Day in and day out in Vienna, the Berrys deal not only with a gang of terrorists (resident on one floor of their hotel) but with a sly, dirty-talking circle of prostitutes (resident on another floor of the place). They're beset both by racists and by enraged victims of racism. They're even obliged to learn how to handle the media. (Lilly Berry's fans, hyped into a condition of hysterical idolatry, are infuriated with her relatives for their unwillingness to cooperate in establishing her as a secular saint.) If, in short, the quality of the children's sense of fun and feeling for each other stands forth as "normal and nice," neither the children's environment nor their individual natures quite warrant those labels. Nightmare and sunshine simultaneously, once again.

A fair question about this pairing is: What's it for? Does juxtaposing the quotidian and the melodramatic—the normative and the eccentric, the healthy and the sadistic—offer much besides shock value? Doesn't it become merely confusing? John Irving's triumph in his last book was traceable, I believe, to the brisk ingenuity with which he dispatched these doubts. *Garp*, as will be remembered, is in part about a novelist and his audience—a novelist plagued, like most, by readers whose interest seems sometimes to derive exclusively from curiosity about whether his stories are autobiographical. The most horrible episode of rape and murder in the book is presented as a chapter of a novel written by T. S. Garp shortly after losing a beloved child in an automobile crash. As one reads the episode, one isn't merely titillated by the grisly and forbidden; one is shown, dramatically, how a writer transforms personal experience into an achieved imaginative narrative that, despite being complexly rooted, in every detail, in "real life," is remote from any set of actual happenings. Graphically depicted sexual encounter becomes, through elegant indirection, a lesson about art and its sources, a means of access to a father's inexpressible grief, and an instrument capable of reconciling totally opposite modes of feeling.

I confess I suspected that this feat—the purposeful linking of the normative and the perverse or hateful—couldn't be brought off a second time, but I was wrong. Less bloody than *Garp*, *The Hotel New Hampshire* nevertheless is rich, from start to finish, in incongruous juxtapositions, and it offers genuine pleasures. I don't pretend to know all of Mr. Irving's secrets, but I'm fairly certain about one of them. Early in the book the reader is nudged into noticing resemblances between the narrative proceedings at hand and those of a fairy tale—the only literary form that has ever satisfactorily tamed the horrible. Half-magical attachments between human and animal creatures (men and bears) hold our attention from the start. John Irving reflects time and again on dreams, wish fulfillment, happy endings. And in the touching final page, he steps forward to acknowledge that he and his reader have been living in a "fairy-tale hotel," spinning wish fulfillments: "We give ourselves a sainted mother, we make our father a hero; and someone's older brother, and someone's older sister—they become our heroes, too. We invent what we love, and what we fear. There is always a brave, lost brother—and a little lost sister, too. We dream on and on: the best hotel, the perfect family. . . ." Guided by the narrator, we intuit that this work (when the grotesque heaves into sight) is not only about the unbearable but about our instinct for refusing the unbearable—not only about the worst of life but about our capacity for willing away the worst. That intuition does much, throughout, to soothe our unease with contortions and contrarieties.

We're also soothed because a good deal of the worst in *The Hotel New Hampshire* really is willed away. A few dread events in the story—a plane crash, a blinding—are irreversible. But, as it turns out, they're exceptions to the book's rule. Brother and sister fall in love and sexually embrace—but their embrace is a means of canceling the memory of the cruel rape: before the end Franny Berry transcends her incestuous passion and her lesbian attachment, and gives herself fully to marriage, procreation, health. Frank Berry, self-absorbed homosexual, is led out of his enclosure into the sunlight of selflessly generous relationships with both siblings and elders. A young woman once so convinced of her ugliness that she went about the world in disguise is helped to discover her beauty, arrives at a positive view of herself, becomes the means through which John Berry conquers his infatuation with his sister.

And as it goes with individuals, so it goes with impersonal forces of negation. The racism and sexism that stalk the opening chapters bow in shame at the conclusion. Blacks and whites come together in harmony that is rooted in perception of their shared humanity. The brutalizing rapist Caliban who attacked Franny understands that he too must alter his ways. And—highly impressive utopian accomplishment—the terrible energy of rape comes to seem less real, less momentous, than the infinitely loving, patient process by which a rape crisis center brings about, in the abused, the rebirth of trust. We occupy, in other words, a world wherein nearly everything comes out as we should like, the formal and psychological sequences moving from tragedy to comedy, from despair to hope. And, to repeat, because we begin to feel, close to the start, the inevitability of that fairy-tale progress, the intermingling of destructive and nurturing elements just escapes the taint of arbitrariness.

An exceedingly dense and clever work, in sum. Conceivably it will provoke attempts—full of humorless posturing outrage, as fatuous in their way as philistine panegyric—to prove the author to be a dollar-maddened opportunist. Writers who seem intent on having their art both ways (Let's see: How about a good salty mix of *The Waltons* and Genet?) are often spanked as opportunists. But that line seems wrongheaded to me. John Irving's love and squalor please us precisely because his authorial presence seems unsmudged by baseness—innocent, cheerful, bouncily energetic, at times incoherent, but always beyond reach of exploitative meanness.

This isn't to say that every objection to *The Hotel New Hampshire* should be discounted. I found a certain frailty in the book's emotional life; feelings such as terror, lust, and *ressentiment* need powerful invocation to be persuasive, and the author's charm and jokey off-handedness—his very fascination with his eye for incongruity—conspire to muffle and miniaturize them. (Grief at the loss of parent or child disappears from the page almost before its weight can be imagined, like an effortlessly cleaned barbell.) I also find the preoccupation with rape, here and in *Garp*, disconcerting. And although the novelist Garp is explicit in warning us off from reviewers who utter such phrases, I'm obliged to declare that John Irving doesn't strike me as a writer of significant intellectual depth. "Everything *is* a fairy tale," says the narrator of *The Hotel New Hampshire* confidently, and I can think of several greatly admired texts (one of them is Heidegger's famous Hölderlin essay, contending that poetical fancy is the foundation of our being on this earth) that develop closely related themes. John Irving, however, seems far more comfortable with obliviousness—with our incapacity for seeing beyond the self-endorsements of culture, class, and enclave—than are the subtlest minds who have celebrated imaginative power. And, for me, his books' frequent allusion to Scott Fitzgerald only underlines the fact that the example of that writer's moral penetration has been missed. Irving's work brings to mind lesser heroes—J. D. Salinger, Kurt Vonnegut, the Beatles.

Like those performers at their best, this author is playful, tender, ebullient, by turns silly and sweet. And, most important, he has within him a strong idealizing tendency, which, at an hour when nothing is more conservatively chic than despising the ideal, deserves regard as precious. His one-man struggle to make the novel safe for—or at least hospitable to—domesticity isn't, I grant, a mark of genius; neither is his effort to persuade us that people caught in the muck of habitual obscenity—or aberrancy or phony liberation—truly want out. But at their core both efforts are kind and sane as well as funny and diverting: everybody smart will know enough to wish them well.

MICHAEL PRIESTLY

Structure in the Worlds of John Irving

A writer subdues the chaos and confusion which is reality by creating order and structure within a world of fiction. In each of his first four novels, John Irving imposes a personal order upon the world within the novel, but his own characters and stories question the tenability of such order. The characters, in their own realm, search independently for their own order.

In his first novel, *Setting Free the Bears* (1968), the two main characters are Siggy and Graff. Both young men search in vain for an explanation of the order imposed upon the world of Vienna. Siggy cannot escape his past, and Graff cannot foresee a future: "We're at an interim age in an interim time; we're alive between two times of monstrous decisions—one past, the other coming. We're taking up the lag in history, for who knows how long." Siggy has had "only a pre-history—a womb and pre-womb existence at a time when great popular decisions with terrible consequences were being made . . . it's the pre-history that made us and mattered to what we'd become."

In response to what he considers a controlled existence in a confining environment, where he is unable to exercise free will, Siggy plans a symbolic gesture of rebellion against the occupation of his world by more powerful forces: he will let all the animals out of the Vienna Zoo. Graff eventually enacts the liberation, after Siggy's death, but the gesture is predictably ineffectual. Like the man he had heard about who had tried the same thing at the

From *Critique: Studies in Modern Fiction* 23, no. 1 (1981). © 1981 by the Helen Dwight Reid Educational Foundation.

end of World War II to protest the occupation of Vienna, Graff realizes that, no matter how well-intentioned, he has been "rendered inert": "What worse awareness is there than to know there would have been a better outcome if you'd never done anything at all? That small mammals would have been better off if you'd never meddled in the unsatisfactory scheme of things."

Despite, or perhaps because of, his inability to effect order on the real world, the narrator, Graff, attempts to impose his own order upon the world in which the story takes place. He takes liberties in how he presents the story itself, over which he has no control; he "meddles in the unsatisfactory scheme of things." Part Two of *Setting Free the Bears* contains Siggy's note-book which is read, edited, and presented to us by Graff. The notebook follows two different but deliberately interwoven stories: Siggy's "highly selective autobiography," which is his pre-womb, womb, and shortly-there-after existence; and the "zoo watch." Siggy wrote the latter in first-person present, presumably in nearly total darkness while creeping around the zoo grounds making plans to let the animals out.

From the second page to the last page of *Setting Free the Bears*, Graff quotes from Siggy's notebook, which he had not yet read at the time the story begins. After he tells us that he has actually read it, he (and Irving, too) explains, in a chapter titled "P. S.," his reasons for including the notebook and why the two parts were interwoven. He then continues to give at least a vague explanation of how the notebook relates to Siggy's life—the writer to his world: "I still feel the two journals demand separation, if only for literary reasons. And certainly Siggy made some obscure connections between his awesome history and his scheme for busting the zoo; though for my own part, I can't speak too well for the logic in that." Graff, as distinct from Irving, plays the naive narrator who is not absolutely sure why he imposed this order upon Siggy's work. Graff narrates *Setting Free the Bears* as a story that he has lived through (as if he has actually had a previous life); in a sense, it is *his* "selective autobiography." As a person, neither Graff nor Siggy had any control over the greater powers that imposed order upon the world of Vienna; but as the narrator, Graff tries to impose his order on a fictional world that he has created by telling the story.

Irving's third novel, *The 158-Pound Marriage* (1974), ends on a distressing note of confusion and helplessness, which is similar to the ending of *Setting Free the Bears* when Graff wishes he had left well enough alone. The unnamed narrator, one of the four major characters, spends the duration of the book trying to understand his world and himself, only to realize that the more he learns, the less he knows: "I knew once again that I knew nothing." The novel is the narrator's attempt to understand and participate in the synergamous affair that has become the structure imposed upon his world. The narrator, who labels himself an historical novelist, is involved with Edith, a writer, who is married to Severin Winter. Winter, a German teacher and wrestling coach at a New England college, is having almost by default an affair with Utch, the narrator's wife, who grew up in Vienna. What the narrator never seems to realize is that both Utch and Edith are deeply in love with Winter; he is merely the pawn in a game of emotional vengeance.

We find out though a series of flashbacks that all four characters lived, for a time, in Vienna—where they met each other. The world within the novel, however, is the world of the relationship between the four. When the structure imposed upon their lives by this relationship becomes untenable, all four character return to the world of "pre-history that made them and mattered to what they'd become." Like Siggy and Graff, the characters of *The 158-Pound Marriage* live in an "interim period": their quaternary relationship is an order that was imposed upon their world after they left Vienna and before they returned to it. As with Graff in *Setting Free the Bears*, we can see through the attempt by the narrator to impose his own order upon his world by telling his autobiographical story selectively. The narrator includes himself in a group of writers (historical novelists) and confesses that "We historical novelists are somewhat hung up on *what if's* of this world." His association with a group perspective, so to speak, provides a key to his view of the relationship he shares with Edith, Utch, and Winter. He observes human activities, plagued by what-if questions. Although he pretends to be objective and removed from the influences of human emotion, as historical novelists might like to believe, he is anything but objective about his situation. That we know he is more emotionally involved and more susceptible to emotional pain than he knows himself makes an important statement about the relationship of a writer to his world, about the way he tries to adapt that relationship to the world of fiction he creates.

The narrator's vulnerability and his semiconscious attempt to ignore it give him a distaste for the "new fiction," a type of fiction which involves no risks to the writer and requires no self-exposure. The writer Helmbart, who appears as a character in both *The Water-Method Man* and *The 158-Pound Marriage*, represents the writer of the "new novel" or new fiction. Helmbart, as a person and a writer, is the key to an understanding of the narrator and how he looks at his world; he is also the key to understanding Irving's relationship to his own world and the worlds of his fiction. In *The 158-Pound Marriage* "the famous Helmbart" is the writer-in-residence at the university where Winter teaches and where Edith takes creative writing courses. Edith tried for a while to work with Helmbart on her writing but eventually decided that "she neither liked his work nor him." Then she began working with the unnamed narrator, who considers himself an historical novelist. He insisted on the term "historical novel," despite the bad connotations it had for people like Edith, because he "felt that novels which did not convey real time conveyed nothing." After working with Edith for a short time, the narrator says: "Helmbart's sort of haughty kingship over what was called 'the new novel' was nauseating to me. Edith and I agreed that when the subject of fiction became how to write fiction, we lost interest; we were interested in prose, surely, but not when the subject of the prose became prose itself."

The narrator also confesses to Edith that he resents being disregarded by the university, which never includes his books on their list of faculty publications. The list includes "Helmbart's fiction, and a rift of the usually scholarly articles—a piece, for example, on the 'Furniture Symbols of Henry James,'" but the narrator has "always felt that there was a greater similarity between these articles and Helmbart's tiny fictions than the respective authors would admit." In *The 158-Pound Marriage*, then, the narrator essentially defends his own work because it conveys a sense of time; his writings are sequential, which implies the lives and emotions of human beings. The narrator denies his own vulnerability, which would be exposed if he admitted to writing about human emotions, by calling himself an historical novelist, and he criticizes Helmbart because he writes fiction about fiction, not about people. At the end of his story, the narrator admits that "I knew once again that I knew nothing" because he realizes his own failure. He imposed his own order on the story by telling it in his own self-deceiving way; but, once finished, he knew that he was still under the control of the order imposed upon his world by greater forces.

Irving's second and fourth novels, *The Water-Method Man* (1972) and *The World According to Garp* (1978), end on more positive, more definite notes. Unlike Siggy and Graff or the characters of *The 158-Pound Marriage*, Bogus Trumper and T. S. Garp achieve their ultimate goal: to impose a viable structure upon their self-contained worlds. Fred "Bogus" Trumper, protagonist and narrator of the second novel, tells his own after-the-fact story of his life as a failure. A former wrestler, student of German and comparative literature at Vienna and Iowa universities, soundtrack engineer for an independent film-maker, and unenthusiastic tyro in writing—Trumper never completes any of his projects, from his wrestling matches to his doctoral thesis—to the raising of his son. Wracked with self-doubts and pained by a deformed urethra (which he tries to cure with the "water method"), Trumper neither understands why his marriage with Biggie fell apart nor why his relationship with Tulpen give him so little satisfaction.

Trumper begins in first-person narrative and tells us that "I'm going to stick to the facts. I want to change." This virtuous resolution is deceptive, because Trumper later reveals that what happened in the first chapter, including his resolution, is what he begins to write at the end of the book. The entire story is Trumper's attempt to recount what he had to go through to impose order upon his own world and, consequently, upon the self-contained world of his fiction that he has created to enable him to tell his own story. Although he switches back and forth from first person to third, depending on the situation, Trumper has written a book about himself writing a book. As in *The 158-Pound Marriage*, "the famous Helmbart" again provides a clue to understanding the structure of the novel. Ralph Packer, the independent film-maker, refers to a review of Helmbart's contemporary novel, *Vital Telegrams*, in an attempt to explain the structure of his new film to Trumper. Packer says that "The structure is everything. . . . The transitions—all the associations, in fact—are syntactical, rhetorical, *structural*; it is almost a story of sentence structure rather than of characters; Helmbart complicates variations of forms of sentences rather than plot." The film is about Bogus Trumper, but the comparison to Helmbart's novel leaves Bogus unable to understand the connection: "What Trumper had some difficulty understanding was what relation Helmbart's world had to Ralph's film. Then he thought of one: perhaps neither of them meant anything. Somehow that made him feel better about the film." What Trumper also had difficulty understanding was the relation between the film about himself and his own life.

Trumper's problem is his "mush-minded ability to read his own sentimentality into everything around him." As a graduate student, Trumper could not finish his thesis, a translation of *Akthelt and Gunnel* from the Old Low Norse, presumably because his sentimentality and vulnerability got in the way. He stopped translating with Stanza 280 because the doom of Akthelt and Gunnel seemed inevitable: "The world was too strong"—for them and for Trumper. As he comes to realize but refuses to admit, Packer's film about him, in its lack of structure and sense of meaninglessness, reflects his own confused, purposeless life. Trumper can impose a structure upon the world of fiction, his story about himself, only after he has imposed structure upon his life. *The Water-Method Man* "is almost a story of sentence structure" and chapter juxtaposition "rather than of characters."

By the end of the book, Trumper has found his own peace and has begun his book, ostensibly about himself, which is *The Water-Method Man*. He has mastered his sentimentality; he has found comic perspective and the complex narrative technique and structure which enable him to write the book; and he has written the book from behind the facade of narration and structure that he has imposed upon his own story. The peace he has found, however, is not entirely a product of his own will: "He used to think that peace was a state he would achieve, but the peace he was feeling was like a force he'd submitted to." A structure had been imposed upon his world by Tulpen, his ex-wife Biggie, and his old friend Couth, who now has a relationship with Biggie—somewhat like the way a structure was imposed upon the narrator's world in *The 158-Pound Marriage*. Irving, like the fictional Helmbart, "complicates variations on forms of sentences rather than plot." By creating a complexly structured world within each of his novels, Irving forces us to follow the tortuous paths of his narratives and to search in every corner of the structural mazes for life-sustaining truth. From the distance of the perspective he has achieved, Irving tells his stories in such a way that we question the plausibility of the "facts" within his fiction.

The Water-Method Man begins: "Her gynecologist recommended him to me." Trumper narrates many of the book's thirty-eight chapters in first-person present. When he describes events that happened before he met Tulpen, the "her" of the first sentence, and before he began the "water method," he narrates in third-person past, as if he were describing someone else—the person he was before he decided to "change and stick to the facts" and straighten out his meatus, an alignment that coincided with the decision to straighten out his life. In Chapter Twenty-seven, "How is anything related to anything else," Trumper begins writing a diary. He manages only one sentence; "in fact, it was a real cliff-hanger of an opening line." It was the same sentence with which he began the book itself. Nor have we seen the last of this sentence. In the final chapter, long after Trumper has given up his one-sentence diary, he sits down to write. This time, having found the peaceful life that he thought he wanted, he writes the same sentence again and manages to add to it the rest of the first paragraph of the book. He could go no further: "What have I begun? He didn't know. He put the paper with these crude beginnings in his pocket to save for a time when he had more to say."

In Chapter Twenty-seven, which includes the analysis by Packer of his new film about Trumper as well as the beginnings of Trumper's diary, Irving provides more than enough clues to enable the reader to understand the structure of *The Water-Method Man*. Irving seems to feel a need for such explanation, the need to provide a key that will liberate the reader from the burdens of analyzing plot and structure. Without the key, the reader would perhaps not persist in seeking out the wisdom and the truths hidden behind the intricacies of the structure and the exaggerations and absurdities of the sometimes vapid characters.

In *The World According to Garp*, Irving's characters become much more individually real, their personalities much deeper and more developed, even though, on the surface, they have passed further beyond the realm of credibility than those in *The Water-Method Man*. The variation on forms of sentences in his second novel becomes variation of plots in his fourth, each serving to illustrate certain aspects of the relationship of a writer to his work, the real world to the fictive. T. S. Garp's world is not the self-contained world created by Irving, but a world within the novel, created by Garp himself. In *The World According to Garp*, the narrator, whose omniscience could bring doubts to the most faithful reader, describes Garp's world in the third person. While Garp, a young writer, searches for a way to write his stories with his imagination and not from his memory, the narrator of the novel has already found the necessary perspective. Garp is a writer whose own world exists only in what he writes, just as the world that Garp tries to survive exists only in what Irving writes.

Within *The World According to Garp* are two short stories, the first chapter of a novel (with a summary of the rest), and the abstracts of two other novels—all written by Garp. The young Garp finds his first inspiration in the "world according to Marcus Aurelius," from an often-recurring quotation. Garp's adopted mentor helps him find his writer's perspective which crystallizes in his third novel, *The World According to Bensenhaver*. In its first chapter (the only one we can read), this novel-within-a-novel proves to be a microcosmic *roman a clef*: the key that unlocks the complexities of Bensenhaver's world also fits the door to the world of Garp.

Young Garp, whose world began without him in the story of his mother, eventually goes to Vienna to become a writer. Vienna is "the city where Marcus Aurelius died," according to the owner of a bookstore where Garp buys an English translation of the Stoic philosopher's writings. According to Marcus Aurelius: "In the life of a man, his time is but a moment, his being an incessant flux, his sense a dim rushlight, his body a prey of worms, his soul an unquiet eddy, his fortune dark, his fame doubtful. In short, all that is body is as coursing waters, all that is of the soul as dreams and vapors." Parts of the quotation surface in Garp's mind at nearly every critical point in his development as a writer. He first experienced "a writer's trance, wherein the world falls under one embracing tone of voice," as he remembered the Marcus Aurelius quotation. When he felt this "trance," he was able to finish his first important short story that had been half-written months before. Garp's story, called "The Pension Grillparzer," is the first place "that we can glimpse what the world according to Garp would be like." Its peculiar characters are products of his unalloyed imagination, but the "dreams and vapors" of his soul breathe life into them to make them real. Through an exaggeration or distortion of the reality that is Vienna, Garp created a small but hermetic world that reflects the truths of human quality that exist in our own.

Garp finished "The Pension Grillparzer" soon after his mother, Jenny Fields, finished her first and only book, an autobiography entitled *A Sexual*

Suspect. We find out later in a reference to his own work that Garp thinks "autobiographical fiction is the worst kind." Throughout his life, Garp struggles between the power of his imagination and that of his memory. When his imagination is in control, he can draw on his own experiences and write brilliantly; when his memory dominates, he can write only "x-rated soap operas" which too closely resemble his own life.

Garp's first novel, aptly named *Procrastination*, was an historical novel set in Vienna during World War II. It was judged a creditable debut but little more. In his next book, *Second Wind of the Cuckold*, Garp's struggle between imagination and memory becomes a serious problem. He builds the plot and characters around a synergamous affair that occurs between him, his wife, and another couple. On the basis of the summary provided, Garp seems to have used his imagination only to add outlandish and bizarre traits to his characters—one is blind, another prone to interminable flatulence, a third spastic. He deceives himself into believing that the novel is not autobiographical, but his wife, Helen, accuses him of self-deception: "You have your own terms for what's fiction, and what's fact, but do you think other people know your system? It's all your experience—somehow, however much you make up, even if it's only an *imagined* experience. People *think* it's me, they *think* it's you. And sometimes I think so, too."

To some extent Irving has here provided himself a literary self-defense. Not only are parallels obvious between his life and his work but between Garp's works and Irving's. *Setting Free the Bears* is partly an historical novel set in Vienna during World War II; *The Water-Method Man* is, in part, a novel about procrastination, the title of Garp's first book. The title of the second, *Second Wind of the Cuckold*, is a play upon a quote from Severin Winter which is repeated by the narrator at the end of *The 158-Pound Marriage*. Although exaggerated by Garp, the basic plot is the same in both books. By fictionalizing autobiographical material and then justifying his perspective within the fictionalization, Irving proffers an explanatory defense of his own work, particularly through his study of Garp's development as a writer.

In a later chapter of *The World According to Garp*, Helen and Garp enjoy one of their favorite bedtime games: Helen tries to guess how much, if any, of the story she has just heard him tell their son is true: "Then he would say to her that it didn't matter; she should just tell him what she didn't *believe*. Then he would change that part. Every part she believed was true; every part she didn't believe needed work. If she believed the whole thing, then the whole thing was true." Garp tries to imagine everything so personally that his imaginings will be as vivid as his memories and will seem, to others and to himself, just as real. His memory, however, often distorts his imagination, and vice versa. He strives for a "*vision* . . . an overall scheme of things, a vision all his own," but to achieve it, he must develop a commensal relationship between his imagination and the real world. Garp wants his fiction to be fiction, not autobiography, particularly when his memories become unrelentingly painful to him. His writing depends on his finding a way to step back from his own terrors, so that he may put his fears and his anguish into his writing before they overwhelm him. By committing his own terrors to words he can, in a sense, watch them die. Garp's need to continue writing and to continue living leads him back to Marcus Aurelius, whose stoicism maintains that a man's "time is but a moment"; he must concentrate on attaining his own personal vision of virtue, not on the "coursing waters" of emotional, mundane life.

The World According to Garp is peopled by an extraordinary cast of characters: rapists, child molesters, transsexuals, Ellen Jamesians, assassins, a slew of people without parents, either for natural or unnatural reasons (Garp's mother, for example practically impregnates herself in a hospital bed with a terminal patient who has reverted to infantile mentality). The book is filled with carefully plotted stories, which become more and more bizarre as the novel progresses. To be a writer in such a world, Garp must find a perspective from which he can create his own world. The world he creates must exist beyond the realm of reality in the realm of imagination; the reader who enters Garp's world must be astounded by its grotesquerie and exaggeration but must also accept the world as a reality in order to find the beauty and truth that lie within.

Several tragic occurrences leave Garp incapable of writing anything but tormented, gory tales that too closely resemble his own unforgettable, torturous memories. In *The World According to Garp*, Garp comes as close as he ever will to finding the perspective necessary to his writing: "Garp knew what terror would lurk at the heart of his book, and perhaps for that reason he approached it through a character as distant from his personal anxiety as the police inspector is distant from the crime." The story, told by a third-person, omniscient narrator, explores the world according to the police inspector, Arden Bensenhaver. Garp wrote the story in this way because he "felt guided by an impulse as old as Marcus Aurelius, who had the wisdom and the urgency to note that 'in the life of a man, his time is but a moment . . . his sense a dim rushlight.'" Garp knew that if his passion or his emotion (kept alive through his memory) gained control of his reason and his sensibility (brought to life by his imagination in the creation of the world according to Garp), he would not only be unable to write, he would be unable to live. Through his imagined creation, Garp could impose the reason and order on an imaginary world that he could not impose on his own very real one.

In the first chapter of *The World According to Bensenhaver*, the inspector investigates a case in which a man who brutally rapes a woman is stabbed to death by his victim. Bensenhaver's deputy, when asked by a passerby if he sees a lot of rape and murder, realizes that "He had never seen a rape or murder before, and he realized that even now he had not actually seen it through his own eyes as much as he'd been treated to the experience through the eyes of Bensenhaver. He had seen rape and murder according to Bensenhaver, he thought. The deputy felt very confused; he sought some point of view all his own." Just as the deputy was confused and in need of a point of view, Garp was confused in his attempt to find a personal view in his writing that would not result in "autobiographical fiction." The relation of Garp to *The World According to Bensenhaver* is analogous to the relation of the narrator to *The World According to Garp*, and the outrageous characters which spring from Garp's imagination are comparable in nature or outrageousness to the characters which Irving creates in his imagination.

In several ways, Irving seems to invite a comparison of Garp and himself, despite Garp's frequent reminders of the danger of such a comparison. According to Garp's thesis on the uselessness of art: "He rejected the idea that art was of any social value at all—that it could be, that it should be. . . . He saw art and social responsibility as two distinct acts. The messes came when certain jerks attempted to combine these fields. Garp would be irritated all his life by his belief that literature was a luxury item; he desired for it to be more basic—yet he hated it when it was." Garp's lifelong conflict with art and social responsibility is inseparable from his conflict between imagination and memory. If his memory prevails, his art becomes more "basic"— he writes about himself, which he cannot bear. If his imagination prevails, his art becomes a luxury to him; he creates a world in which everything lives according to him. The degree to which *The World According to Garp* is autobiographical fiction, characters and events coming directly from Irving's life, matters very little. Of greatest import according to Irving or the narrator is the degree to which *The World According to Garp* is a product of imagination. Irving draws on the things he knows and the places he has been to create a fantastic, bizarre world in which all the characters are still infrangibly human: their feelings, actions, and basic personalities are not warped, twisted aspects of the superficies—they speak truth from the heart. We cannot accept the outrageous absurdities of Garp's world only because Garp himself cannot: he must create his own personal imaginary world of escape to enable him to survive in a world that he cannot control.

Two aspects of *The World According to Garp*, however, are problematic: the narrator's penchant for epigrammatic quotations, and his refusal to let the lives of his characters end. From the "pre-historic" beginning of the book, before T. S. Garp has seen the light of day, the narrator chides us with supercilious commentary that Garp presumably wrote: "As Garp wrote of his mother's dilemma: 'Her colleagues decided that she felt herself to be superior to them. Nobody's colleagues appreciate this.'" Also from the beginning of the story, we find out what will happen later to nearly every character in the book, two- to three-hundred pages before it happens. After all the events have occurred, some of them twice, we find out in a lengthy epilogue what will happen sometime around the year 2000 to everyone who is left. The epilogue, "Life After Garp," is added for the purpose of "'warning us about the future,' as T. S. Garp might have imagined it." Why are these quotations and the epilogue included? One explanation is that Irving uses them to remind us of the unquestionable omniscience of the narrator, who is intended to be Garp's official biographer: he has created this world and he knows what is going to happen because the entire book exists in his mind. He began writing the book after Garp had died.

In Garp's words, the act of starting a novel is like "trying to make the dead come alive. . . . No, no, that's not right—it's more like trying to keep everyone alive, forever. Even the ones who must die in the end. They're the most important to keep alive. . . . A novelist is a doctor who sees only terminal cases." The novelist's cases are terminal because he knows they must die, and he knows when they will die; but until then, the novelist (or the novelist *cum* biographer) must describe them as vividly and personally as if they were really alive. Exaggeration and distortion of characters and their lives have a certain value because these qualities force the reader to search for the truths imperiled within such a world, truths betrayed to the reader by the essential humanness of the characters. But the quotations and the epilogue threaten to shut the reader out of the narrator's self-contained world by removing it to the realm of the nineteenth-century romance or even to a futuristic fantasy of life after Garp, into which the reader can escape without qualms of conscience about the applicability of Garp's world to the present reality.

John Irving's first four novels suggest that to him structure is *nearly* everything. All his novels are structurally complex, and they all incorporate remarkably similar settings and experiences, somewhat like those in Irving's own life. Writers, former wrestlers, New England colleges, Vienna, Iowa—we find them in all the books. Similar characters appear in all four works, and the same characters also appear. The same aging but elegant Viennese prostitute, for instance, with a fur muff to hide her sparkling ringed fingers, appears in *The Water-Method Man* and *The World According to Garp*—only her name has been changed. Yet these novels are worlds apart, as different from each other as their main characters are from the author. Irving uses his own experiences ruthlessly to create self-contained worlds within each novel—

worlds of exaggeration populated with bizarre, sometimes absurd characters—in order to compel us to recognize the truths that underlie human existence. Regardless of the world in which we find them, the truths Irving
magnifies are unchanging.

Certain aspects of his works suggest that Irving has not yet achieved his
goal of writing a novel whose structure does not to some degree obfuscate his
stories, and a story whose exaggerated effects do not to some degree negate
the validity of the truths he wishes to expound. Irving has imposed an order
upon the world in each of his novels which enables the character to live.
Graff and the narrator of *The 158-Pound Marriage* attempted to impose their
own order upon their worlds; by the end of their stories, both realized that
such order was artificial and temporary and would not hold. Trumper and
Garp both found peace; with it they found a perspective that enabled them
not only to survive a "world that was too strong" but to create their own
worlds by finding a way to write fiction about themselves. Like Garp, Irving
has been trying to find a personal vision, a way to tell his stories with his
imagination and not his memory. In a large sense, the narrative techniques
and perspectives that Irving employs in his first three books are all included
in *The World According to Garp*, but the narrator in that novel is omniscient,
unlike the others who are involved in the stories they narrate. Each of the
earlier narrators presents a "selective autobiography," a story told through
his own perspective, while the narrator of *The World According to Garp*
presents a "selective *biography*," a story about a world and its inhabitants to
which the narrator is virtually unrelated and about which he presumably has
learned through such sources as Garp's unpublished writing.

The World According to Garp is the closest that Irving has come to
writing a selective autobiography—which is important in one very strong
sense. By exaggerating events and characters from his life, Irving has made
them more interesting and better adapted to his own needs. He has found
both his personal vision and celebrated its arrival in *The World According to
Garp*. Through an omniscient narrator, Irving has imposed order and structure upon the "lunacy and sorrow" of the world within the novel—just as
Donald Whitcomb has in his biography of Garp, and as Garp has in his
writing, which is actually the "world according to Garp." Irving achieved the
distance he needed to write a nonautobiographical story, just as Garp eventually did when he wrote *The World According to Bensenhaver*, even though he
could not totally divorce himself from the book. Garp explains the writer's
relation to his work and the relation of his characters to their worlds through
the inspector's deputy who "had seen rape and murder according to Bensenhaver" but "sought some point of view all his own." In a similar way, Irving
explains his relation to his work through a detailed study of Garp as a writer,

through the progressive development of a writer whose works are not, at least conceptually, unlike his own, and through all of the detailed justifications for how and why he turns events and persons from his own life into fiction.

A fine line can be drawn between writing fiction about fiction and writing fiction about writing fiction. In each of his works, Irving examines the relationship of a writer to his work, but he does it principally through describing the writer's life, not his work. Irving's fiction is obviously not the fiction of a Helmbart—the kind of fiction associated with the French "new novelists," such as Robbe-Grillet, Duras, and even Beckett. Despite his remonstrations and attempts to espouse traditional literary values, Irving has up to now written a combination of modern and traditional fiction. In *The World According to Garp* he combines traditional story-telling and literary modes (chronological sequence, omniscient narration, and the epilogue) with modern techniques (writing-within-writing and self-reflexive narration). All four of his works contain writing which Irving uses to explain his own intentions and explicate his own text.

Like the village explainer, Irving seems to feel a need to justify his own narrative perspective in telling a story. He has not quite been able to divorce himself from the academic world—in which the didact who tells a story to make a point then explains his point to make sure no one has missed it. In explaining himself, Irving resembles both the Victorian novelist ("dear reader") and the "new novelist" who writes fiction about fiction. In each of his novels, he has imposed a structure upon his fictional world; his characters, then, explain the structure, question its validity, and proceed to search for a new structure, a personal vision of their own. John Irving is perhaps still not satisfied with the perspective he has attained; he has stated that his next work, *Hotel New Hampshire*, will be a linear story—without any writer-characters. *The World According to Garp* may be the end of only the first leg in his journey towards finding his own personal vision, in a life where "his time is but a moment."

ROBERT TOWERS

Reservations

I was decidedly a late-comer to *The World According to Garp*. Over-urged by enthusiasts in the summer of 1978, I became resistant and did not even make a start on the novel until it had appeared in its rainbow assortment of paperbacks. Then I had trouble getting past the first chapter, which seemed to me unbearably facetious in its account of the engendering of T. S. Garp by a ball-turret gunner lobotomized by shrapnel and a nurse who hated sex. The prospect of more than 400 pages of jokey contrivance, weird sex, and eye-gouging details of physical horror was off-putting; I have always disliked a kind of hyperkinetic fiction in which a proliferation of "vividly" written incidents is made to do the work of a sustained engagement with a complex and thematically charged action.

But on my third try I reached the scene where the young Garp ventures on to the steep roof of the Steering School to catch pigeons with a lacrosse stick, and I kept going, seduced at last by the suppleness and energy of the writing and by the vision (as much comic as doom-laden) of imminent peril that henceforth irradiated the narrative. Though there were still sections in which sensationalism got out of hand and became exploitative, I felt that Irving's inventiveness was on the whole matched by a depth of commitment to his material and that mere contrivance was kept at bay almost until the end by a tender and passionate concern with Garp's family life and his career as a writer.

From *The New York Review of Books* 28, no. 17 (5 November 1981). © 1981 by NYREV, Inc.

Though Irving's earlier novels prefigure in various ways the themes that later engage him, they do not prepare the reader for the sheer abundance of *Garp* or for the superb display of narrative self-confidence with which the author directs his characters in their vaudevillian turns. For the sake of a writer's career, such a performance should ideally be followed by a very different kind of a book, one that would not constantly invite comparison with its remarkable predecessor. Irving obviously had other intentions, for he has made it almost impossible for anyone familiar with *Garp* to read *The Hotel New Hampshire* without constant cross-referral to the former. But before venturing further into the matter, I had best give a short account of the new novel for the sake of those tardy readers who have not yet caught up with the numerous reviews and copious publicity attending its publication.

The Hotel New Hampshire is essentially the story of an oddball New England family, the Berrys. The parents are Winslow and Mary, both born in 1920, and the children include Frank (a grumpy, prudish boy who is incidentally homosexual), Franny (an outspoken, foul-mouthed, reckless, and warm-hearted girl), John (the novel's narrator, who goes in for wrestling and weightlifting), Lilly (an exceptionally serious child who stops growing at an early age), and Egg (a little boy who loves costumes). Win's father, a philosophical football coach called alternately Iowa Bob and Coach Bob, and a vile-smelling old labrador called Sorrow are also members of the household. The novel begins with a rather charming and nostalgic flashback to the courtship of Win and Mary, who both have summer jobs at a resort hotel in Maine in 1939; there they encounter an Austrian animal trainer named Freud and his aging black bear known both as "Earl" (from the sound of his growl) and "State o' Maine." Win buys the bear and gains the hand of Mary. Almost at once they begin producing their peculiar brood. The section ends with the death of old Earl, shot by a "dumb kid" who did not realize that the bear was somebody's pet.

We leap ahead to the mid-Fifties. Win Berry, who has a fixation on hotels, quits his job as a prep-school teacher and converts a former girls' school into the first Hotel New Hampshire. The eccentricities of the hotel's staff, its furnishings (chairs from the former schoolrooms still screwed to the floor, tiny toilets and washbasins designed for very small girls, etc.), and its guests (among them a circus of dwarfs) are fully equal to those of the Berry family, who take up residence there. The fourteen-year-old John has an affair (limited to rainy mornings) with a blowzy waitress. Franny is gang-raped by three "ringers" on the prep-school football team, led by an icily arrogant boy named Chipper Dove to whom she is perversely attracted; subsequently she is comforted to some degree by another teammate, a powerful and kindly black whose sister had undergone a similar experience. Smelly old Sorrow and Coach Bob meet their untimely ends. Sorrow is stuffed.

The next move carries the family all the way to Vienna, where Win, at the instigation of the old animal trainer Freud, takes over the management of a decrepit hotel and renames it the Hotel New Hampshire. But by this time the family is missing two more members, for Mary and little Egg perish in a plane crash en route to Vienna; Sorrow, whose stuffed body was being carried along by Egg, floats to the surface of the sea. In Vienna we resume our acquaintance with old Freud, now blind, and meet another trained bear, who acts as Freud's seeing-eye and as a kind of bouncer at the hotel; the bear also speaks English, for she is in fact an unhappy, tough-talking, good-hearted lesbian named Susie, a Sarah Lawrence dropout who has taken to wearing a bear suit. There is much, much more: a terrorist plot to blow up the Vienna State Opera; the return of the now-famous Berrys to the United States, and the sudden emergence of tiny Lilly as a literary success; an episode of sibling incest; an elaborate revenge on Franny's rapist, Chipper Dove; the purchase of a third Hotel New Hampshire. . . . But enough has been given to indicate the extraordinary whimsicality of this novel and to suggest, to those who have read *Garp*, the many links connecting the two books.

Among these are incidents involving (in no particular order) performing bears, rape, mutilation, seedy Viennese hotels, Viennese prostitutes, wrestling, and sudden death. While reading *The Hotel New Hampshire*, I had to pause repeatedly to ask myself how a particular motif had been played before. What was achieved by the new variation? What, indeed, was Irving's purpose in constructing this Wagnerian nexus of subjects, images, and themes extending from one novel to the next? Take the matter of rape. "I feel uneasy," Garp wrote, "that my life has come in contact with so much rape." We are told that Garp himself would later write a novel which would have much to do with rape. Meanwhile, in *Garp* itself, we are subjected to harrowing accounts of the rape of two pre-teenage girls (one of whom, Ellen Jamison, has had her tongue cut out) and the attempted rape-murder of a young wife.

In *The Hotel New Hampshire*, not only Franny but also Susie the bear is a rape victim. There is much dialogue on the subject, Susie being particularly eloquent. "Those thugs didn't just want to *fuck* you, honey," she says to Franny, "they wanted to take your strength away, and you let them. . . . Sweetheart! You have *minimized* the *enormity* of what has happened to you—just to make it a little easier to take," To which Franny protests, "Whose rape is it?... I mean, you've got yours, I've got mine. . . ." And there is still a third victim in the novel—Sabrina, the beautiful young black woman who instructs John Berry in the art of kissing; she, we are told, was not only raped but had all her teeth knocked out. At the novel's end the third avatar of the Hotel New Hampshire is transformed into a rape crisis center directed by Susie the bear; as such it parallels the refuge for distraught women set up by Garp's mother Jenny in the preceding book.

Are we to assume that the rape of defenseless young girls, especially if accompanied by mutilation, has some special poignancy for Irving, arousing some private guilt for which repeated fictional atonement must be made? Presumably not—though both Garp and John Berry are made to go on at length about their abhorrence of the crime. It seems more likely that he is playing an elaborate literary game, teasing the reader with hints of profound continuities underlying metamorphosis—Ellen Jamison is, after all, a rein-carnation of the mythic Philomela and so, in thicker disguise, is Sabrina. Meanwhile, the multiplication of rapes has furnished no further insight into the nature—or the consequences—of sexual abuse. So it is with the other repetitions. We are invited to take part in a game called "Count the Bears," beginning with the "liberation" of those truculent, shambling, unpre-dictable mammals from the Schönbrunn Zoo (*Setting Free the Bears*); we can observe them riding motorcycles in both *Garp* and *The Hotel New Hamp-shire*, and in the latter we can actually watch one of them undergo a non-Ovidian metamorphosis into a truculent, lovably growling human female. The bear motif and the rape motif are joined when Susie, wearing her bear suit, threatens Franny's terrified rapist (Chipper Dove) with rape by a sexu-ally aroused bear. But the significance of neither motif has been enhanced, and the whole episode is about as funny (or profound) as a fraternity initia-tion in high school.

Again and again *The Hotel New Hampshire* disappointed me by the perfunc-toriness of its situations and their handling. That quality of jokey contrivance which initially put me off in *Garp* is painfully in evidence throughout the new novel. When, during an electricity blackout, an elderly patrolman switches on the ignition of his squad car at the very moment that the power comes back on, lighting up every window in the hotel facing him ("*as if he had done it*") and startling the old cop into a fatal heart attack, we may smile at the joke and register once again Irving's predilection for sudden death; when, fifty pages later, Coach Bob, the philosophical grandfather, suffers a fatal heart attack at the unexpected sight of the stuffed dog Sorrow falling out of the closet, we are more likely to respond with an exasperated shrug. The incident has been too blatantly set up, made too predictable. How often can one be expected to respond to the play on the name Sorrow, which runs through much of the book? The nature of Coach Bob's death is clearly intended, in turn, to underscore the thematic seriousness of the following exchange—a flashback—that occurs a dozen pages further on:

> And one night, when we were watching a wretched melo-drama on the TV . . . , my mother said, "I don't want to see the end of this. I like happy endings."
> And Father said, "There are no happy endings."
> "Right!" cried Iowa Bob—an odd mixture of exuberance and stoicism in his cracked voice. "Death is horrible, final, and frequently premature," Coach Bob declared.
> "So what?" my father said.
> "Right!" cried Iowa Bob. "That's the point: So what?"
> Thus the family maxim was that an unhappy ending did not undermine a rich and energetic life. This was based on the belief that there *were* no happy endings. . . . Franny and I were probably believers of this religion—or if, at times, we doubted Iowa Bob, the world would always come up with something that seemed to prove the old lineman right. We never knew what Lilly's religion was (no doubt it was a small idea, kept to herself), and Egg would be the retriever of Sorrow, in more than one sense. Retrieving Sorrow is a kind of religion, too.

So much for the tragic vision of life. The passage is typical of the prevailingly juvenile tone of the novel, which is full of the bittersweet wisdom of a late-hour bull session interrupted from time to time by exploding firecrackers.

Events of potentially great impact (young John's sexual initiation by the much older waitress, the death of Mary Berry and Egg) are summarily treated, as if the mere statement that they have occurred will stimulate an appropriate (and automatic) response from the reader. Characters are for the most part glibly sketched in or else sentimentalized, as with the brave, handsome, generous, and sexy black athlete, Junior Jones, and his sister Sabrina; only Franny seems to me successfully realized as a character, made touching by her boldness and vulnerability. A speeded-up, shorthand treatment of character and situation of course works in certain types of comic writing but not in a novel of such length and pretensions.

The "throw-away" attitude toward the material is matched by the slackness of the style. Succumbing to what Henry James saw as a dangerous "looseness" inherent in first-person narration, Irving allows his John Berry to go on and on, dully including quantities of inert and unredeemed detail.

Ronda Ray, cruising the dance floor, spotted Frank behind the empty tables, but Frank fled before she could ask him to dance. Egg was gone, so Frank had probably been waiting for an excuse to go corner Egg alone. Lilly was dancing, stoically, with one of Father and Mother's friends, Mr. Matson, an unfortunately tall man—although, if he had been short, he couldn't have been short enough for Lilly. They looked like an awkward, perhaps unmentionable animal act.

Father danced with Mrs. Matson and Mother stood at the bar, talking with an old crony who was at the Hotel New Hampshire nearly every night—a drinking friend of Coach Bob's; his name was Merton, and he was the foreman at the lumberyard. Merton was a wide heavy man with a limp and mighty, swollen hands. . . .

Nowhere in *The Hotel New Hampshire* does the language have the confidence, the aphoristic precision, and the vivacity that are among the pleasures of *The World According to Garp*. As if aware of the stylistic inadequacies of the new book, Irving resorts to the use of literary crutches, quoting at length from the poems of Donald Justice and from the famous conclusion of *The Great Gatsby*, which makes Lilly burst into tears and declare that their father is a Gatsby, always in pursuit of the receding green light. The very rhythms of the end of *The Great Gatsby* are echoed in the final paragraphs of *The Hotel New Hampshire*: "So we dream on. Thus we invent our lives. . . . We dream on and on: the best hotel, the perfect family, the resort life. And our dreams escape us almost as vividly as we can imagine them." Unfortunately, the quotations and echoes serve only to emphasize the lameness of Irving's own prose.

In this review I have, almost at the novelist's invitation, used a good book—*Garp*—to belabor a poor one. Enough. John Irving is a talented and resourceful writer. I doubt that he has been misled by the hoopla, cover stories, etc., surrounding his latest production. I like to think that next time he will present us with something as exciting as *Garp*—and as different from that novel as he can possibly make it.

JOSEPH EPSTEIN

Why Is John Irving So Popular?

"Ambushing a Best-Seller" is the title Edmund Wilson gave to a 1945 review of a novel by Anya Seton, but clearly it is too late to ambush the novelist John Irving, who has already ridden into town, cleaned out the banks, and ridden out again unharmed. After publishing three novels, Irving rang the bestseller gong, and rang it with a sledgehammer, with his fourth, *The World According to Garp*, and then rang it yet again with his fifth and most recent novel, *The Hotel New Hampshire*. These books have not been bestsellers merely but thunderous bestsellers. Three-and-a-half million paperback copies sold of *The World According to Garp*, weeks and weeks atop the bestseller lists for *The Hotel New Hampshire*, *Garp* soon to be a movie. . . .

Yet all this is matter best left to the accountants. What is more interesting, what distinguishes John Irving's recent novels from the regular run of even thunderous bestsellers, is that they are not books meant for entertainment alone. They are written out of serious intentions, and by and large they are read in a serious way by their varied audience. My sense is that this audience is fairly youthful, Irving's readers ranging preponderantly between their early forties and their early twenties, though not exclusively so.

John Irving's admirers take his novels seriously, he most certainly takes them seriously, but how seriously ought serious people to take them? Fifty million Frenchmen can't be wrong, they used to say before the establishment

From *Commentary* 73, no. 6 (June 1982). © 1982 by the American Jewish Committee.

of the Vichy government; can five or six million American readers of John Irving? Of course they can, and over questions of serious art large audiences generally are wrong. Yet they need not necessarily be. Right or wrong, however, the wide readership for John Irving's novels—mainly youthful, mainly middle class—is itself a phenomenon worth considering in its own right. But before considering the phenomenon of Irving's commercial success, let us consider the products that made the success a phenomenon— the novels themselves.

"Jubilant" is the word Mordecai Richler used to describe the quality of John Irving's talent. "America's most jubilant bestseller" reads the blurb atop the paperback edition of *Garp*. Jubilation, surely, is one of the effects Irving seeks as a novelist—a sense of joyousness, of exultation. Fittingly, he is a high-energy writer, who works in heavy brush-strokes, goes in for colorful effects, does not write the kind of careful novel in which, as Virginia Woolf once said of the novels of Jane Austen, "one slip means death."

In the contemporary novel, jubilation also implies comedy, comedy of a somewhat manic kind, and Irving, from the very beginning of his career, has been a comedian. The character T. S. Garp says, "Why did people insist that if you were 'comic' you couldn't also be 'serious'?" I am not sure that many people do insist this, for it is fairly common knowledge that there is a comedy that is at bottom highly serious. More about the quality of John Irving's comedy presently, but for now let it suffice to say that, as with the work of so many contemporary American novelists—Pynchon and Barthelme, Elkin and Roth, Coover and Barth—Irving's is riddled, is fairly bristling, with comic scenes.

Sex, too, is central to the Irving novel. Fancy fornication in one form or another is never far off in any of John Irving's novels, and it ranges from adolescent sex to lesbian love to couple-swapping to incest. Fellatio in a car, both moving and parked, is another Irving *spécialité de la maison*. Comedy and sex often combine, and the result is generally scenes that are frenzied, hysterical, madcap, shading into slapstick in which lust leads to an Irving hero being caught *in flagrante delicto*. The centrality of sex in these novels is curious, in that Irving often goes well out of his way to make plain his hatred of the sexual exploitation of women and his sympathy for the general tendency of their liberation from the old regime under which, presumably, women were treated as sexual objects. More than one of John Irving's novels manages to be both liberationist and pornographic. But then sex is perhaps the only one of life's activities where one can eat one's cake and have it, too.

The physical side of life generally gets a great deal of play in the novels of John Irving. Sweat, secretions, smells, bumps, lumps, rumps—all come in for their share of descriptive prose. Although Irving is fecund in imagining incidents for his characters to run through, it is apparently a bit more difficult for him not to create a narrator or at least one principal character who is, as they say in the locker room, "in shape." Wrestling, running, weightlifting; physical conditioning of one strenuous sort or another is, in a way that is not quite made explicit, connected to spiritual conditioning. But then perhaps the joggers of our day do not need to have the connection made any more explicit.

One needs to be in a certain shape oneself to read a John Irving novel; rather a strong stomach, specifically, is required for the violence that is integral to his novels. Characters are set upon by bears and other wild animals; body parts drop off people with a more than fair regularity; bombings and rapes are provided; a character from Irving's first novel, *Setting Free the Bears*, meets his death through suffocation in a pit of human excrement, and he, mind you, is a sympathetic character. In a notorious scene in *Garp*, a car crash results in the loss of the following human inventory: one child, the eye of another, and one penis. But this is lyrical stuff compared with another scene in the same novel in which (in the course of a story within the larger story) a man is disemboweled while committing a rape. John Irving is not unaware of the heavy dosage of violence in his novels, and in his latest, *The Hotel New Hampshire*, his narrator remarks of the book's ending, "I know it's not nearly violent enough to please some of the friends and foes from our past. . . ."

It was only with the fourth of his novels, *The World According to Garp*, that John Irving began to talk thus to his readers, to refer to his own works within his works. Roughly three-quarters of the way through *Garp*, for example, Garp, the narrator, tells us that he is planning to write a novel called *My Father's Illusions*, which turns out to be not the title but one of the principal themes of Irving's next novel, *The Hotel New Hampshire*. In *Garp*, too, the narrator is supposed to have written an earlier novel entitled *The Second Wind of the Cuckold*. Irving never wrote such a novel, though the phrase—"If cuckolds catch a second wind, I am eagerly waiting for mine"—is found embedded in the last line of Irving's previous novel, *The 158-Pound Marriage*. One autobiographical parallel follows another in Irving's recent novels, and these are often followed by little sermonettes about the need to disregard "shitty autobiographical associations that make those rabid readers of gossip warm to an occasional fiction." And again: "Usually, with great patience and restraint, Garp would say that the autobiographical basis—if there ever was one—was the least interesting level on which to read a novel." Setting down a rug, then pulling it out from under a reader, this is what academic literary critics, who are infinitely patient men and women, like to call novelistic playfulness.

Although no doubt Irving would detest the notion, there is a strong sense in which he is an academic novelist. He is a former student at the University of Iowa Program in Creative Writing, and while you can take the boy out of the Program in Creative Writing you can't always take the Program in Creative Writing out of the boy. Two of Irving's five novels—*The Water-Method Man* and *The 158-Pound Marriage*—have academic settings. But more is involved than scenes and settings. In the very first of Irving's novels, *Setting Free the Bears*, which has to do with freeing the animals from the Hietzinger Zoo in Vienna, one already senses certain school-learned touches, bits, ironies. Having set a good part of this novel during World War II, Irving has one of his characters remark late in the novel, that his teacher, a Jew, "was enraged that I should be so pretentious as to dash through the war with so little mention of the Jews. I tried to explain that he should really look at my autobiography as what is loosely called fiction—a novel, say." Irving often goes in for these Chinese-box effects—character are writing books or shooting films within his books—and this game-playing, rather than telling a story straight out, is one of the standard marks of the academic novelist at work.

More important than John Irving's academic roots, however, is that his writing seems very much of a special generation. In *Setting Free the Bears*, Siegfried, the hero of the novel, who in 1967 is twenty-one years old, remarks: "What I mean is, we're at an interim age at an interim time; we're alive between two times of monstrous decisions—one past, the other coming." This quotation may make John Irving seem a political writer, but he isn't, at least not in any obvious or direct way. What he is, I think, is a generational writer—a writer attractive to readers of a certain age. It is the young—or rather the youngish—to whom he appeals. His novels exert their greatest pull on those people who are undecided about growing up; they are college-educated, getting on and even getting up in the world, but with a bit of the hippie-dippie counterculture clinging to them still—yuppies, they have been called, the initials YUP standing for young urban professionals. A friend who is a professor at my university's law school, for instance, recently told me that many of the younger law professors among his colleagues are nuts about the novels of John Irving. Not that this constitutes a CBS/New York *Times* poll, but I have never before heard of young law professors being nuts about any novelist. Why? What's the attraction?

Irving's second novel, *The Water-Method Man*, is about a graduate student in German at the University of Iowa, who only reluctantly accepts the roles of husband and father. Fred "Bogus" Trumper is his name, extreme passivity his game. The passive hero, or hero as passive, has by now become a tradition of sorts in contemporary American fiction. We have had a Dangling Man and an Invisible Man, and to these Irving adds a Water-Method Man. The title refers to a method of treatment that the novel's hero undergoes for the difficulty he has in urinating: drinking lots and lots of water. *The Water-Method Man* is the most convoluted of Irving's novels—his hero is doing a translation of an old German epic for his dissertation, while at the same time a documentary film is being made of his life—and also easily the most boring. A great many little academic games are being played out in it: dead ducks appear, people sleep with tropical fish tanks around them, the hero retells the story of *Moby Dick* to his child—in short, there is plenty of symbolism to go around.

Certain elements appear in the pages of *The Water-Method Man* that will be hallmarks in John Irving's novels to come: the broad joke is carried a bit beyond much too far (the squeamish are advised to pass up the urological jokes and horror stories that run throughout); the rather persistent dropping off of human body parts begins in earnest; the hero turns out to be a wrestler; the main characters arrive, as they invariably do in an Irving novel, in Vienna; adorable children appear who must be protected from the world's cruelty; and, finally, there is a celebration of the flesh (the last clause in the novel reads, "Bogus Trumper smiled cautiously at all the good flesh around him"). And, too, as with all of Irving's novels, whatever the suffering and death that have gone before, the ending is somehow upbeat. But then wasn't it William Dean Howells who said that what the American public wanted was above all a tragedy with a happy ending?

The 158-Pound Marriage is Irving's best-formed novel. Its subject is wife- and husband-swapping, with an occasional bout of *ménage à quatre* and a single detour into lesbianism. Of the four principals, two are writers, one a teacher and wrestling coach, one an Austrian brought up by a captain of the army of the USSR during the occupation of Vienna. It is the most sex-ridden of Irving's novels, even though at one point its narrator says that "sex is only a temporary cure." In the pages of *The 158-Pound Marriage* it has to do until something better comes along. Nothing better does. Reading this novel one is inclined to agree with one of the two wives, who near the close, remarks, "I think we were just *f—ers!*" Something new has been added for the first time in Irving's work, an element that will henceforth appear in all his novels; for the first time discussions of fiction appear in the middle of his fiction. "Edith and I agreed," the narrator says, "that when the subject of fiction became how to write fiction, we lost interest. . . ."

Mutilation of various kinds continues in *The 158-Pound Marriage*. Men without legs, a man with a hole in his face, a dancer with a part of her foot missing supply some of the novel's notable subtractions; children are also wounded in a blood-drenched shower-door accident, but afterward, if memory serves, all parts are present and accounted for. At this point in one's reading in John Irving's novels one begins to wonder about all these wounds, rips, tears, broken bones, and vitiated organs. There arises the question, to adapt a phrase of Henry James's, of the disfigurement of the carpet.

It did not arise too urgently because John Irving's standing as a novelist was not itself an insistent question. His first three novels gave him the reputation of an interesting but minor writer. ("Garp," thinks the hero of Irving's next novel, "*hated* the reputation of 'small but serious.'") Commercially, he appeared to be one of those novelists who would eventually have to be published by an outfit like the Fiction Collective. Then, in 1978, along came *The World According to Garp*, a success both critical and commercial. People not only bought this, Irving's fourth novel, they read it; they not only read it, they loved it. "Joyous and outrageous," wrote the critics, "full of vitality and grace," "rich and humorous," "brilliant," "overwhelming," "superb," "wonderful," "absolutely extraordinary."

Extraordinary *The World According to Garp* is. So loaded down with incident and invention is the novel that its plot beggars recapitulation. Briefly, it is an account of the life and times of a youngish novelist, T. S. Garp, the fatherless son of a well-born woman who, quite without consciously wishing it, becomes a feminist leader and heroine. Garp's wife is a university teacher, who teaches among other things a course in narrative technique, but it is Irving who attempts to show how much technique a narrative can have. His novel contains two separate short stories and the first chapter of another novel, *The World According to Bensenhaver*, which will make Garp himself a hugely bestselling novelist, even as, we now know, *The World According to Garp* made John Irving a bestselling novelist. Bears, wrestlers, Austria, by now old Irving standbys, put in their appearances. Instructions about writing and book reviewing are provided between bouts of sex (and sex, for Garp, "was always an act of terrific optimism"). Garp quotes Marcus Aurelius one moment, and the next—most unAurelianly—tups one of his childrens' babysitters. Mutilation fans will not be disappointed. One of the principal characters in the novel is a former tight-end for the Philadelphia Eagles who has had a sex-change operation. A group of militant feminists—the Ellen Jamesians—cut out their tongues. ("But Garp . . . felt the whole history of the world is self-mutilation.") There is a bit of couple-switching, also an assassination. The novel has an epilogue, in which two characters agree that "Garp was a man with remarkable energy."

The World According to Garp is not so much salted as drenched in sex and violence, but so is the world drenched in sex and violence, and so, too, in recent years have a large number of novels been drenched. The sex and violence in *Garp* do not, in any case, go very far toward explaining the novel's immense popularity, for these are to be had in ample supply elsewhere. In *The Water-Method Man* a passage runs: "You should always tell stories . . . in such a way that you make the audience feel good and wise, even a little ahead of you." This implies that a bestseller can be rigged, but here, too, there are reasons for doubting, for if it were so easily do-able it would be done more often. In the pages of *Garp*, Garp's editor feeds his authors' manuscripts to a cleaning woman at his publishing firm: "She did not like most things, but when she said she liked something, it meant to John Wolf [the editor] that nearly everybody else was at least sure to be able to read it." A valuable woman, clearly, every publishing house ought to have one, but I fear she exists only in John Irving's imagination.

No, when a book such as *The World According to Garp*, a book with serious literary pretensions, catches on so epidemically with the public, something else, something deeper than pat formulas for constructing best-sellers is involved. In the recent book *Bestsellers*, which investigates the popular fiction of America and England during the 1970's, John Sutherland makes the point that vastly popular novels need to be considered from two points of view, the economic and the ideological. The economic has to do with the way a book is marketed. Of the ideological, Sutherland writes: "The bestseller expresses and feeds certain needs in the reading public. It consolidates prejudice, provides comfort, is therapy, offers vicarious reward or stimulus. In some socially controlled circumstances it may also indoctrinate or control a population's ideas on politically sensitive subjects. In other circumstances, especially where sexual mores are concerned, it may play a subversive social role."

"Ideological" has to be understood here in its loosest sense; certainly it does in considering the case of John Irving, for Irving is not, in any reasonable sense of the term, a radical or ideologue. On the contrary, in his novels he has demonstrated real disdain for people whose lives are controlled by their politics: the Ellen Jamesians in *Garp* and a group of Austrian radicals in his more recent novel, *The Hotel New Hampshire*, are equally detested by their author. The ideological freight carried by John Irving's recent novels is not, then, political in the strict sense, but is instead to be found in Irving's attitudes, point of view, what he himself calls his vision.

The young T. S. Garp, considering his own early writing, thinks: "What I need is *vision*, he knew. It will come, he repeated to himself. . . ." Has John Irving's vision come? His novels are an extraordinary jumble, of the sentimental and the violent, of the cute and the loathsome; reading them one sometimes feels one is reading a weird collaboration between J. D. Salinger and John Hawkes, a strained effort to be, simultaneously, adorable and gruesome. In *Bestsellers* John Sutherland says that bestselling fiction tends to divide ideologically between the emancipated (Erica Jong, for example) and the traditional (James Michener, for example). In a strange yet evidently commercially successful way, John Irving's latest novels tend to combine the emancipated and the traditional, the effect of which is to make his readers feel advanced in their views yet fundamentally sound in their emotions.

For instance while disdaining the wilder side of women's liberation in *Garp*, Irving views it very kindly. As a writer, T. S. Garp stays home, does the cooking and cleaning, and is generally, not at all to his displeasure, the model house-husband. John Berry, the narrator in *The Hotel New Hampshire*, plays, quite comfortably, a roughly similar role in that novel. Yet the one character is an ardent wrestler, the other a serious weightlifter—traditionally masculine, one might even say *macho*, types. John Irving prides himself on his endless invention—"Garp," he writes, "was a natural story teller; he could make things up, one right after another. . . ."—but his real invention is in the creation of these heroes. They are extremely sensitive (Garp lies down next to his young son to smell the freshness of the boy's breath in his sleep), yet when it is required of them, brutally tough (John Berry, in *The Hotel New Hampshire*, kills a man with a bearhug). These John Irving heroes, these sweet bruisers, are also permanently puerile, young men whose chief experience occurred in adolescence—it's downhill after your middle-teens, says a character in *The Hotel New Hampshire*—and who have been able to arrange things so that, whatever their chronological age, they never quite have to leave adolescence.

The Hotel New Hampshire has ridden high upon the bestseller lists for better than half a year now. The New York *Times*, in a capsule comment on the book in its bestseller list, describes it as "Life with an eccentric family." That description as aptly fits *The Brothers Karamazov*, so perhaps a better one might be, "Winning formula well in hand, John Irving strikes again." Although Lily Berry, the daughter of the family in this novel who is herself a bestselling novelist says, "My God, the next book has got to be bigger than the first," in fact *The Hotel New Hampshire* is not quite so vast in its canvas as *The World According to Garp*. It is about a family whose father harbors utopian illusions about running a hotel that will provide perfect hospitality, hospitality with slight psychological overtones. "People have to grow their own way," Father says. "We provide the space." Many of the same symbols and themes, incidents and concerns, appear here as in *Garp* and Irving's earlier novels: the Austrian interlude, the bears, the physical conditioning, the sidebar discussions of fiction ("Life is serious but art is fun"), the mutilations.

The appeal, too, is similar. At the heart of this novel, as of *The World According to Garp*, is the allure of family.

As in *Garp*, so in *The Hotel New Hampshire*, family becomes a fortress of a kind into which one withdraws with one's children for protection against the cruelty of the world. Rape, in both novels, is a big item (". . . rape, Garp thought, made men feel guilt by association"). Rape is indeed at the very center of *The Hotel New Hampshire*; the rape and recovery from rape and revenge for rape of Franny Berry are the incidents that bind the novel together. At the novel's close, the narrator and his wife—formerly a lesbian so homely she preferred to go about in a bear costume (I'm not making this up; John Irving did)—move into a final hotel that they use as a rape crisis center.

The Hotel New Hampshire is pro-family and anti-rape. If these views do not simply take your breath away, let me go on to say that in all of John Irving's novels, discerning good from evil is never a problem; like every other moral question, it never really comes up. There are good folks and there are bastards in these novels, and one hardly needs a program to tell one from the other. Good folks can go under, but bastards get it in the neck—and in the nether regions. ("It was not one of Garp's better points; tolerance of the intolerant.") As the narrator of *The Hotel New Hampshire* puts it: "The way the world worked was *not* cause for some sort of blanket cynicism or sopho- moric despair; according to my father and Iowa Bob, the way the world worked—which was badly—was just a strong incentive to live purposefully, and to be determined about living well." Now here is advice your local young law professor and a happy few million others can live with comfortably.

GABRIEL MILLER

The Good Wrestler

*T*he *158-Pound Marriage* is Irving's most corrosive work, and also his most self-consciously literary one, exhibiting a marked departure from *The Water-Method Man* in its treatment of character and in its tone. Once again, he examines the ways that people have of destroying each other, although this time, the marriage relationship is given almost exclusive focus—we are outside the realm of history invoked in *Setting Free the Bears* and that of the individual crisis which was the primary concern of *The Water-Method Man*. In this work, the saga of Akthelt and Gunnel is given contemporary treatment, with a less violent though still brutal outcome.

Irving's third novel remains linked to his others in its overt concern with novelistic form and design; however, Irving abandons here the multiple narrative technique to present the entire novel in the first person. His narrator juggles with chronology, manipulating his audience by holding back some essential information during certain sequences and filling it in later. The form is, nevertheless, basically chronological, although this tendency does necessitate occasional abrupt transitions from the present into the past. This novel also continues to deal with places, motifs, and themes common to the earliest works: Vienna, the male protagonist's protective obsession with his children, the aloof father figure; fidelity/infidelity; and sudden, shattering violence.

Irving's comments on the origins of this novel are revealing:

From *John Irving*. © 1982 by Frederick Ungar Publishing Co.

49

> I got this idea for a literary novel: given the company I was
> keeping—and I mean the books I was reading, too—that was
> understandable. *The 158-Pound Marriage* is about two couples—
> a sexual foursome—and it grew very specifically out of Ford
> Madox Ford's *The Good Soldier* and John Hawkes' *The Blood
> Oranges*. If I'd not read those two books, I would not have written
> *The 158-Pound Marriage*. That's the kind of period I was in at the
> time: everything I read was a *labor* and it made me *angry*. It was
> like I lost my sense of humor.

This novel is indeed deeply indebted to both Ford and Hawkes; Irving even
quotes a passage from each novel as a double epigraph (a device he has not
used before or since). All three novels share a basic plot structure, involving
the interrelationship of two married couples, although Irving's book is
perhaps closer to Hawkes's in its almost exclusive focus on the couples and
their decision to swap mates. (Ford's novel concentrates on a love triangle,
with a fifth party actually being more involved in the novel's action than one
of the couples.) Briefly, *The 158-Pound Marriage* revolves around two international couples: the narrator, an American historical novelist, finds himself
attracted to an American woman who has hopes of becoming a writer,
whereas her husband, a professor of German (employed at the same university as the narrator) and wrestling coach, finds in the narrator's wife another
Viennese victim of World War II. The novel explores the past lives of these
characters prior to their marriages and the history of the sexual experiment
that they undertake.

    The three novels are all narrated in the first person by a central male
participant in the action, and Irving combines in his work aspects of both
of the earlier narrators' functions. In Ford's *The Good Soldier*, Dowell's
narrative is, in part, an attempt to piece together what he calls "the saddest
story I have ever heard" and so come to an understanding of it. This has
always been one reason for Irving's use of first-person narrative, providing
his characters the opportunity to review their lives and to place them in
some kind of perspective—Siggy's journal is a first-person account
(though here history is the subject to be sorted out), as is Fred Trumper's
review of his past life. Irving's (nameless) narrator in this novel also seeks
to comprehend both the nature of the complex relationship in which he
has become involved and his own part in it. Yet this narrator wants more
than simple understanding, and in this respect he is nearly related to Cyril,
the "sex singer" and narrator of Hawkes's *The Blood Oranges*, for both characters endeavor also to justify their actions and behavior in the dramas
they are describing. Both characters try, through their narratives, to slant

their tales to their own advantage (as Dowell does not). Hawkes's narrator, however, "spins his tapestry" in an attempt to win back Catherine, his partner in the game of love, whereas Irving's narrator has no such desire— his narrative is merely an attempt to assimilate the experience and thus to justify himself.

The Blood Oranges and *The 158-Pound Marriage* are further likened by the two central male characters, Hugh in Hawkes's novel and Severin Winter in Irving's, whose essential distrust of the love experiments they enter upon injects notes of fatality and doom into the enterprises, and who play significant roles in the destruction of their respective affairs. In both novels the narrators fail to understand or come to grips with these antagonists; their narratives, in part, attempt to discredit them.

The makeup of Irving's two couples is interesting in its relationship to the two couples in *The Good Soldier*. Irving's couples, as mentioned earlier, are both international; during the course of the novel, the two Americans come together, as do the two Austrians. Ford, on the other hand, pits an English couple against an American couple, not involving them in an exchange of mates, though Florence Dowell (the narrator's wife) is for a time the mistress of Edward Ashburnham, the novel's central protagonist. Dowell himself enjoys no illicit sexual favors. The interesting link is in the novelists' attitudes about Americans and Europeans: both identify a vast cultural chasm between the experiences and the sensibilities common to natives of the two worlds. Ford's Americans are rootless and shallow—Dowell, himself an American, exposes his countrymen's endemic vulgarity when he tells of his wife's uncle, who took with him on a world's tour thousands of California oranges to give as presents to strangers:

> For, to every person on board the several steamers that they employed, to every person with whom he had so much as a nodding acquaintance, he gave an orange every morning. And they lasted him right round the girdle of this mighty globe of ours. When they were at North Cape, even, he saw on the horizon, poor thin man that he was, a lighthouse. "Hello," says he to himself, "these fellows must be very lonely. Let's take them some oranges." So he had a boatload of his fruit out and had himself rowed to the lighthouse on the horizon.

The Americans in Ford's novel seem unable to penetrate beneath life's surfaces, and their actions are thus either absurd or, in the case of Florence Dowell, selfish and evil. Irving, too, creates American characters who seem inadequate beside the Europeans. Severin Winter and Utch (the narrator's wife) have been tempered by their experiences as victims of war, which have given them a depth of understanding that the narrator and Edith (Severin's wife) cannot match. The Americans, here as well, are selfish, thoroughly carnal, and unable, as the narration makes very clear, to deal with complexities of feeling and thought.

Irving's novel breaks with its predecessors, however, in matters of tone and theme, and though enriched by the associations, it stands up very well on its own. *The Good Soldier* is a "sad story" that flirts with tragedy but does not achieve it; Ford's protagonists, Edward Ashburnham and Nancy Rufford, withdraw by suicide and insanity (respectively) from a world which they perceive as horrible. The background of Ford's novel, published in 1915, is pervaded by ominous tensions of the approaching World War, a cataclysm that ushered in the modern world, crushing in the process the traditional values of a simpler age. The suffering that Ford's characters endure is reflective of this external calamity; in a world bereft of meaning, the gestures of these figures have a dire absurdity about them.

Hawkes's milieu, conversely, is one of the imagination, for his characters inhabit not a realistic locale—although in *The Blood Oranges*, Illyria is given just enough verisimilitude to veil its metaphoric nature—but a world created of words and art. Cyril, the narrator, finds in his imagination, the medium of his "word weavings," a haven, a point of stability, a refuge: "in Illyria there are no seasons." What takes place in this timeless setting, brought into being by an artist, is a confrontation of life forces—Eros, personified primarily by Cyril, and Thanatos, personified by Hugh. In an interview, Hawkes remarked that "I wanted to create characters in total purity and to deny myself the novelistic easiness of past lives to draw on," and his characters do exhibit a kind of metaphoric purity, as they confront each other as elementary opposites in a dialectic of life and death, time and timelessness. This statement also points up the major difference between Hawkes's narrator and Ford's—the former is an artist, the latter a diarist.

The 158-Pound Marriage, however, is a comic tale about freedom and responsibility, in which the narrator himself learns nothing. Unlike Ford, Irving is not writing about the decline of one order and its replacement by an empty, immoral one, for his universe is one in which the givens are spiritual and moral emptiness, chaos, and violence. He takes for granted, albeit sadly, that man is in a state beyond redemption and that such concepts as faith and ideology, which may have once governed the world, are no longer viable—are, indeed, absent. Irving's European experience and his study of history no doubt fed and elaborated his own basic sense of the all-consuming power of atrocity. Irving's novel is thus, as much as Ford's, manifestly a product of its time: World War I cannot be dissociated from *The Good Soldier*, and *The 158-Pound Marriage* cannot be considered apart from the 1960s, the time frame of its major action and the sphere of its moral climate.

Irving's characters inhabit a grotesque black-comic universe, where a spirit of anarchy prevails and no moral or spiritual values remain to stabilize their lives. To some extent Irving shares the view of the modern French dramatists of the absurd, who believe, in Martin Esslin's words, that "the dignity of man lies in his ability to face reality in all its senselessness; to accept it freely, without fear, without illusions—and to laugh at it." *The 158-Pound Marriage* presents a Dionysian world of almost unrestrained freedom in which human passions—"natural" agents far more terrifying than bears—have been set free. Irving's own judgment of this world is implied in the transparent selfishness of his narrator, certainly the most amoral central character in all of his fiction: a historical novelist who has learned nothing from history.

Unlike Hawkes, Irving requires that his drama be played out in the real world. Committed to the aesthetic values of verisimilitude and mimesis, and to the tenets of traditional plot construction and characterization, Irving has no use for imaginary settings, nor for "pure," archetypal characters—his people have detailed pasts, and history directly affects their lives. Time here is not the abstract concept vaguely perceptible in Hawkes's world, but a very specific and almost tangible force. Whereas Cyril in *The Blood Oranges* seeks to sidestep time, to avoid it as his one true enemy, Irving's characters are always preoccupied with it, recognizing a reality too important to ignore. Rather than attempting to deny the passage and effects of time, as Hawkes's narrator does, Irving's characters actually construct their fictions in order to substantiate it. For Irving, as it were, the narrator remarks, "Novels which did not convey real time conveyed nothing."

If Bogus Trumper is a portrait of someone who manages, finally, to accommodate that part of himself which craves freedom to an overriding sense of the limitations of freedom and of the need for personal responsibility and commitment, the narrator of Irving's third novel represents the opposite reaction. He even recognizes some of his own inadequacies, pinpointing his major problem when he writes: "You can tell a lot about someone by how he deals with insomnia. My reaction—to insomnia and to life in general—is to give in. My best-trained senses are passive; my favorite word is *yield*." In some ways he is like the Rare Spectacled Bears, "passively sad but accepting anything."

More important, however, is that, although he is a historical novelist, he has no perspective. Early in the narrative he correctly points out, "History takes time; I resist writing about people who are still alive". Yet he does just that in the story that unfolds. A second comment is even more ironic, in light of his performance here: "For history you need a camera with two lenses—the telephoto and the kind of close-up with a fine, penetrating focus. You can forget the wide-angle lens; there is no angle wide enough." All of Irving's novels demonstrate the falsity of that statement, as does the narrator's own narrative in this one. The "wide-angle lens" may not, indeed, be wide enough, but it is the business, the fundamental responsibility, of real historians—and Irving insists that all serious thinkers are such—to attempt a broad perspective; any true understanding must be "wide-angled." The narrator, unfortunately, inclines to the more limited focus, interpreting his story only from the "close-up" range, and he is so obsessed by his experiences that it colors his response to even the most unrelated phenomena. Musing about the wartime decapitation of the carved stone figure of an angel on the facade of the cathedral at Reims, he writes,

> It's commonly said in that part of France that the moral of "The Smile of Reims" is that when there's a war on, and you're in it, don't be happy; you insult both the enemy and your allies. But the moral of "The Smile of Reims" isn't very convincing. The good people of Reims haven't got eyes for detail like mine. When the angel has her smile and head intact, the saint beside her is in pain. When her smile and the rest of her head leave her, that saint—despite new wounds of his own—seems more content. The moral of "The Smile of Reims" according to *me*, is that an unhappy man cannot tolerate a happy woman.

Such myopic exegesis—amusing as it may be—is indicative of the view the narrator takes of everything in the novel, his interpretation of events continually skewed by the anger and bitterness of his own involvement and by a fundamental lack of comprehension. Although his narrative continually implies that all essential information has been included, the faultiness of his perceptions makes of his tale-telling a complex and possibly deceptive business.

This narrator very much resembles Hawkes's Cyril in appearance: he is tall and thin, has a beard, and describes himself as "a woman's man." Most important, like Cyril, he is unable to come to grips with his own shortcomings. At one point, Cyril claims that "it is hardly a fault to have lived my life, and still to live it, without knowing pain"; pain, death, and darkness are embodied in Hugh, in whose "dry mouth our lovely song became a shriek." Similarly, Irving's narrator's main antagonist, Severin Winter, is described as dark (as is Hugh), and one who "could pervert the most frankly innocent erotic things."

Severin Winter's history, like that of each of the other central characters, is detailed by the narrator in a chapter headed "Scouting Reports."

Severin's roots are in Vienna, and the descriptions of his parents echo *Setting Free the Bears*: his mother was the actress Katrina Marek—it was under a poster bearing her likeness that Zahn Glanz abandoned his cab—and his father, Kurt Winter, was a minor expressionist painter who managed to get his pregnant wife out of Austria on the day before the *Anschluss*. Severin then grew up fatherless, never really knowing the fate of his lost parent—he is one of three Irving protagonists to grow up without a father (the others are Siggy and Garp). Trumper and the narrator of this novel both have cold, distant fathers, and the narrator's father will die at the end of the novel. Severin speculates that his father, who was full of revolutionary fervor, drove the radical editor Lennhoff to Hungary—Zahn Glanz, too, was credited with this feat—and that twelve days before the Soviets captured Vienna, let the animals out of the zoo. He remarks, "My father loved animals and was just the right sort of sport for the job. A devout antifascist, it must have been his last act for the underground." This link makes Severin Winter part of a gallery in Irvin's world who are intimately acquainted with the essential need for freedom, though Severin stands out as one who understands its implications and limitations. He combines the qualities of Siggy's romanticism—he is also linked to Merrill Overturf in that he once drove a Zorn-Witwer automobile—and the tempered understanding which Graff and Bogus Trumper acquire. Severin is an older man; he is also a father whose romanticism has been assimilated in a positive way—children always force Irving's protagonists to attempt some control over their lives.

Severin was raised by his mother, first in London, where he was born, and then in Vienna; she became an artist's model and the subject of many erotic paintings, many of which hang in Severin's bedroom After his mother's death, Severin was befriended by two Chetnik freedom-fighters who had fled Tito and who were also Olympic wrestlers. They encouraged Severin to go to college in America, where he attended the University of Iowa, majoring in languages and wrestling. As a wrestler, he was once a runner-up in the middleweight class of the Big Ten Championships; wrestling remains for him a central metaphor for life, and one that recurs repeatedly in the novel, as the narrator regularly cites his terminology.

Returning from America, Severin resettled in Vienna, and there met his wife Edith, the daughter of wealthy New Yorkers, who was traveling in Europe and hoping to become a writer. Requested by her mother to find some minor modern European paintings for a museum's collection, Edith went to Vienna to look up Severin Winter, the custodian of his father's art collection. Anxious to sell some paintings to raise money to leave Europe—"Everyone and everything is dying here."—and go back to America, Severin became her guide. Soon they fell in love, and then married and honey-

mooned energetically in Greece: "They made love in the morning, sometimes twice, before getting up. They went to bed soon after the evening
meal, and if making love made them too wide awake, which it often did, they
would get up, go out again and eat another supper. Then they'd make love
again." This youthful Severin is clearly a passionate and active young man—
Edith once describes him as a "baby bear"—but he is not the same man
whose personality dominates the novel's present action.

Closely linked to Severin, both in the experiences of her past and in her
basic attitude toward the *ménage à quatre*, is the narrator's wife, Utch. Like
Severin, she was born in 1938, the year of the *Anschluss*; at the age of three,
she, too, lost her father—also thought to be a revolutionary, he was executed
as a Bolshevik saboteur—and was raised by her mother. Her early childhood
was shadowed by war, punctuated by the necessity of seeking shelter from the
Allied bombings of a munitions plant nearby her home.

When the Russians invaded Austria in 1945, Utch, in her husband's
words, "learned patience." Aware that the occupying troops were looting the
country and raping its women, Utch's mother devised an ingenious plan to
protect her daughter:

> Going over to the largest cow, whose head was locked in its
> milking hitch, she slit the cow's throat. When it was dead, she
> unfastened the head from the milking hitch and rolled the cow
> on her side. She cut open the belly of the cow, pulled out the
> intestines and carved out the anus, and then made Utch lie down
> in the cavity between the great cow's ribs. . . . She closed the slit
> belly-flaps of the cow around Utch like a curtain; she told Utch
> she could breathe through the cow's carved-out anus.

Utch stayed inside the cow's belly—it seems a grotesque variation on Anne
Frank's hiding place—until she was discovered by a benevolent Russian
soldier, Captain Kudashvili. Shortly after her rescue, she learned that her
mother had been raped and killed.

Thereafter, Utch grew up in a Russian sector of Vienna, protected by
Kudashvili and by members of the Benno Blum gang—the "most notorious
criminal gang in Vienna . . . responsible for the 'disappearance' of that
famous one-third of the anti-Soviets in Vienna"—until the Russians
departed in 1955. When Kudashvili was killed during the Hungarian
uprising against the Russians a year later, Utch was left orphaned again.
She remained in Vienna, studied languages (including English), and found
translating work. She met her husband, the narrator, while she was
conducting English tours in the Kunsthistorisches Museum—like Edith,
the narrator married his tour guide.

About his own past the narrator tells very little. His father, a history professor at Harvard for thirty-six years, is distant, and his son called him "sir." He does not seem to take any real interest in his son's career; his mother, however, is a fan of her son's books. (The narrator writes that "as a rule, mothers are more serious than fathers," and this holds true in Irving's universe, although the children of these "absent" or dead fathers generally become obsessive parents themselves—the narrator is an exception.) In 1963, the narrator received a Ph.D. and decided to write a novel based on Bruegel's painting *The Fight Between Carnival and Lent*. Traveling to Vienna to see the painting, he met Utch.

These four character come together at a New England university, where the narrator and Severin are professors. They all meet one night at a dinner party and thereafter develop the bizarre mate-swapping relationship that changes their lives and provokes the narrator's attempt to account for the experience.

The central conflict in the story is between the two men; the narrator blames Severin for the eventual deterioration of the double affair because Severin exhibits a dimension of severity and conservatism that proves ultimately destructive to the relationship. The dichotomy between Severin and the narrator is best epitomized in Bruegel's painting, a copy of which hangs in the narrator's kitchen: Carnival's representative is pictured riding on a wine barrel and brandishing a spit with a pig on it in the direction of Lent, who is thin and drawn and is warding off Carnival with a shovel on which are two herrings. In the painter's characteristic detailing, Carnival is surrounded by revelers indulging themselves in eating, lovemaking, and theatrical performances, whereas good deeds, such as almsgiving, praying and burying the dead, are performed around Lent. Predictably, the narrator's description of the painting emphasizes the Carnival details, and he sees himself as the rich burgher figure in the right-hand corner: "I am moving from the church toward the inn; this seems wise." Bruegel's painting is more balanced: clearly virtue is on the side of Lent, but the outcome is still undecided. Many of the figures on the Lent side of the painting are not sympathetically drawn, and there is a balance to the composition that seems to suspend judgment. Most important, prominent in the center of the painting is a couple, viewed from behind, being led off by a fool. Where are they going? What does this mean? Irving's narrator does not even mention them.

The Carnival/Lent opposition between the narrator and Severin Winter is not so clear-cut. Although Severin is a sobering influence on the couples—his name, like others in Irving's fiction, is playfully allusive—he is by no means a personality of Lenten virtue. He agrees to the exchange of sexual partners because he feels that he owes it to Edith; he had an affair some years earlier, and his agreement is his way of making things even. But

Severin is difficult. Even at the beginning of the relationship the narrator writes, "it was Severin who could never give the four of us a chance. . . . He was uncomfortable, so he tried to make us uncomfortable too." In a central episode, when the couples decide to spend an orgiasic weekend on Cape Cod, Severin sees it as "just a holiday," and cautions, "We should be careful no one gets too excited." He sums up his feelings when he speaks of the futility of having "a little nothing relationship": "I mean, if you have one good relationship, why would you be interested in having a little nothing of a relationship?" Later he adds,

> "I honestly admit the degree of independence that I *don't* have if I live with someone . . . and I expect whoever's living with me to do the same." (Later I remember him yelling: "There's a precious amount of having-one's-cake-and-eating-it-too shit going on around here.")

Whereas Severin does present a troubled, responsible reaction (strengthened somewhat by the narrator's presentation of it) to the sexual exchange, he is not a wholly admirable character. He is nearly related to Bruegel's presentation of Lent, which implies that false piety is no better than dissolute living—beyond the narrator's biased account, Irving's novel thus preserves the balance of Bruegel's painting. The inescapable facts are that Severin has had an affair and that he does agree to the *ménage à quatre*. Also, he hurts Utch by merely going through the motions with her while she falls in love with him. As this duplicity demonstrates, Severin, too, is an egocentric and selfish man. His acquiescence in the mate swapping, further, stems primarily from his discomfort at Edith's being one-up on him on the register of infidelity. Real equality in a sexual relationship upsets him: prior to the exchange, he mentions to Edith one morning that he is thinking of having an affair, and when she admits to having the same thoughts, he becomes angry. He is extremely vain, according to the narrator, "too vain to be jealous," and this is true. His unemotional, almost clinical, involvement in the *ménage* becomes disturbing and tends to balance the sympathy-producing aspects of his announced scruples.

Part of Severin's problem is his inability to free himself of his mother. At one point the narrator comments, "I think Severin thought about his mother too much"—his bedroom in Vienna and later his bedroom in America (after his marriage) is decorated with paintings of his mother in various erotic positions, masturbating. Intimately connected with this is Severin's love for the wrestling room, his own private world. It is described as a womblike enclosure, safe from the reality of the world. It is in the wrestling room that he meets and courts Audrey Canon—it is this affair which precipitates the *ménage*. Audrey Canon is a former dancer who lost part of her foot in an accident; Severin thinks that she is beautiful and claims her "beauty was in her grace, which was in her past. He claimed that he could love a person's past." His preoccupation with the past, and with Audrey Canon's "grace" links her in a way with his mother, an Oedipal connection that Severin cannot seem to overcome. Severin's affair with Audrey Canon ends when Edith finds them in the wrestling room—later she will discover that he has taken Utch there as well. Significantly, both of Severin's wrestling-room lovers are linked to the past—Utch to Austria, Audrey to his mother.

The wrestling room (like Cyril's Illyria) exists for Severin as a kind of imaginative construct, a place where he can be his ideal self, a place where reality does not intrude. Here he can live a strange and, to him, sensual dream, divorced from the world that he finds alien and hostile. In this light a comment he makes about his children is important:

> He said they were his substitute for an adventurous, explorative life. With children his life would always be dangerous. . . . He said his love for Edith was almost rational (a matter of definition, I suppose), but that there was nothing reasonable about the way he loved his children. He said that people who didn't have children were naïve about the control they had over their lives.

This is a typical Irving protagonist's attitude toward children, but it also reveals something relevant to Severin's other involvement: for him the *ménage* is dangerous because he cannot control it. There are too many separate lives involved. That is why his wrestling-room seems safe for him; it is a one-on-one situation, like the sport of wresting itself. But in the four-way affair, Severin does not know how to exercise control. The narrator writes: "I have seen how his wrestlers look at their opponents with a cold, analytical scrutiny, a dead eye. Severin Winter gave me such a look. Though he couldn't have been oblivious to the ridiculousness of his controlled behavior, he cherished the idea!" It is this very idealistic quality about Severin that makes him difficult to deal with, and makes the continuation of the affair impossible.

Only when Severin goes back to the wrestling room—like Plato's cave—can he revert to a baser state. He himself understands this analogy, for his wrestlers enact Plato's parable of emerging from darkness to light before each match:

> He looked them all up and down, as if he could see in the darkness. "*Wie gehts?*" he'd ask them; in the tunnel, his voice boomed.

. . . They were all his German students, you see.

And in unison the wrestlers would bellow in that tunnel, "*Gut!*"

Then Winter would fling open the door, and like moles emerging into daylight, his wrestlers would blindly follow him into the new gym and startling light and yelling crowd and out onto that shining crimson and white wrestling mat. To the spectators they always looked as if they had been brainwashed in a dungeon and sent out on some grim task into the real world. They *had*.

It is Winter's desire to return to the wrestling room—the cave is for Plato a place that keeps out the light of the sun—that counterbalances his idealism. In the dark room a wrestler can regress to a purely physical state, where, as Severin says, "If you think, you realize you can lose—and you're right."

In this light, three events that befall Severin near the end of the novel are particularly significant. Each year he takes his best wrestlers to a championship meet at Oklahoma State University. This year his star, George James Bender, wins all of his preliminary matches and then becomes inexplicably listless and loses his final match. It is eventually revealed that Edith tried to seduce Bender and that "he just didn't get up for it." He was so humiliated that he was unable to wrestle well the next day—Bender's experience with the light of the real world has destroyed his cave mentality. After this episode, Severin resigns as wrestling coach.

During a dinner party with the narrator and Utch sometime later, the Winters' children are badly cut when the glass door of a bathtub falls in on them. This is the central violent episode of the novel:

> The bathroom looked like the scene of a gang-land slaying. The old door had pitched into the tub and broken over the naked girls, the glass exploding from the frame, sending shards and fragments flying everywhere; it crunched under Severin's shoes as he plunged his arms into the tub. The tub was pink, the water bloody; you could not tell who was cut where.

In resigning as wrestling coach, Severin has given up the world of the cave and restated his claim to the world outside. However, in Irving's universe the light of the outside is not the ideal described by Plato in *The Republic*, but a world in which there is no control, where "danger is everywhere." The children's accident enforces this fact upon Severin, while also serving, as such violence regularly does in Irving's fiction, as a punishment for his (and Edith's) faithlessness.

Severin's final act is taking Edith to the wrestling room, in which symbolic act his darker self is sublimated and he renews his connection with the more responsible part of his nature. He seems ready now for a life of commitment to his wife and to his family. The healing process having begun, Severin then joins his family in Vienna, a place where he once learned the lessons of danger, but also a place where truces "run long and deep."

The character who suffers most from the whole experience is Utch. Like Severin, she is a child of pain and suffering, but the affair further scars her, and at the end she leaves her husband and goes to Vienna with her two sons. The narrator has remarked that his wife "could teach patience to a time-bomb," her childhood experience having taught her that. When she came to America with her husband on the day of President Kennedy's assassination, she alone remained unaffected: "In Europe of course, they kill their aristocracy all the time, but not in America. . . . For Utch, I suppose, it was not at all unusual; it was the way they would settle scores in Eichbüchl. Nobody had taught her to expect any other part of the world to behave differently." Unlike the Americans in Irving's world, who are continually surprised and shocked, Utch has learned the lessons of history first-hand, and she is better able to apply this long-range perspective to her own life than her husband, who only speculates about history and its meanings.

Unfortunately, despite the fact that her past is well detailed, Utch does not emerge as a convincing character during the course of the novel. Things seem to happen to her—she mostly gets drunk and falls asleep—though she does rouse herself to fall in love with Severin Winter. Their relationship is largely a matter of speculation, owing to its development beyond the range of the first-person narrator, but it seems likely that their similar backgrounds must have led to a degree of natural understanding and sympathy of feeling greater than she has ever found in her husband. By the end of the novel she has come to understand her husband as well, however, and when the affair is over she dismisses their marriage bitterly with the remark that "You know *you* . . . that's all you know." Thus Utch, who was made so vivid a figure in the account of her childhood experience, presents once again, as she decides to leave her husband, a strong and definable impression, but the effect is not consistent throughout the novel, as her thoughts and responses in the midst of the affair remain too sketchy to convey her development in character. It is a serious flaw in a book whose central focus—and considerable achievement, in the cases of the other three principals—is dynamic characterization.

The narrator, as mentioned earlier, learns nothing; unlike any of Irving's other protagonists, he remains too preoccupied with himself to gain any useful perspective on the experience he has been reviewing in his narrative. He never achieves the "wide-angle view." Despite the fact that he provides the perceptive reader enough information from which to draw some conclusions, the narrator himself cannot seem to piece this information together meaningfully. His summary description of Bruegel's painting and his presentation of his own story demonstrate that he can gather facts and that he has a perceptive eye for detail, but his understanding is so limited that he remains ignorant of the larger patterns of his own life. By the end of the novel, his family has left him and his father has died, but he feels nothing. He concludes the novel with characteristic insouciance:

> Yesterday Utch wrote that she saw Edith sitting in Demel's eating a pastry. I hope she gets fat.
> So. Today I bought a plane ticket. My mother gave me the money. If cuckolds catch a second wind, I am eagerly waiting for mine.

Presumably he will learn little in Vienna, either.

The 158-Pound Marriage is a very consciously styled novel, rich in literary and artistic allusions, and narrated by a writer who occasionally comments on the art of writing itself. In one of his discussions of fiction with Edith, he mentions a colleague who is also a novelist:

> . . . Helmbart's sort of haughty kingship over what was called "the new novel" was nauseating to me. Edith and I agreed that when the subject of fiction became how to write fiction, we lost interest; we were interested in prose, surely, but not when the subject of the prose became prose itself.

He speaks here for Irving, who is a strong advocate of the traditional novel. However, the narrator/Irving is hedging here just a little, for although this novel is a traditional novel—concerned with real time, character development, and plot—it is also very modern in its concern for the fictional process itself. Much of its complexity derives from the manipulation of its narrative by two separate novelists: the narrator and Irving himself, and whereas this dual structuring provides some of its most interesting effects, it is also the novel's central weakness. Irving simply fails to employ the first person consistently; too often the narrator seems to be speaking directly for Irving, from outside his own personality—this was also noticeable in Siggy's journal in Part Two of *Setting Free the Bears*, wherein the reflections on history clearly emerged from a different mind than that reflected in the Siggy of the earlier section. Irving does not seem to possess, in these early novels, the discipline to sustain a first-person narrative by leaving the telling to his character.

When this narrator is discussing Austrian or Russian history, he, too generally lapses into Irving's voice:

> On July 9, 1945, the Allies quartered the city of Vienna for occupation. The Americans and British grabbed up the best residential sections, the French took over the markets and the major shopping areas, and the Russians (who had long-term, realistic plans) settled in the worker-industrial districts and within the Inner City, nearest to the embassies and the government buildings. During the carving of the great game bird, the dinner guests revealed their special tastes.

Again, when he recounts Kudashvili's leaving Utch to fight in Hungary:

> It was the good people of Budapest who freed her. On October 25, 1956, a lot of people's good intentions were upset. The Hungarians did not feel that because Russia had liberated them from the Nazis they owed the Russians anything as unreasonably large as their country.

This tone is very close to that in many of the passages in Siggy's journal; it is even more out of place here because Irving has made it clear that the narrator does not have the perception to write this way about history. This inability to sustain his narrator's voice, which constitutes this novel's major flaw, will at last be corrected in *Garp*, another novel about a novelist, in which Irving will revert to the third person and set off Garp's writing in special sections which interrupt the main narrative. Here, however, Irving comes closer to Helmbart than he may realize, flirting playfully with reflexivity, while yet maintaining his essential allegiance to traditional form.

Another of the novel's weaknesses is the constant reliance upon wrestling metaphors, as the narrator adopts them from Severin's speech. Occasionally amusing, they recur too frequently to function as an effective, or even illuminating, literary device. The title of the novel derives from this tendency, and it is (rather obscurely) significant in terms of the novel's central theme. In college, it seems Severin wrestled in the 157-pound class (later raised to 158 pounds), which is the middleweight category. Wrestlers, however, do not compete at their natural body weights, but at lower weights maintained by constant dieting and exercise; the loss of pounds does not affect muscle strength, which thus becomes a great advantage in the lower weight classes. In other worlds, the wrestler exists in a constant limbo world, striving to combine a weight that is not natural with a muscle strength that is, and fighting in a weight class which thus does not reflect a measurable reality.

The characters in the novel occupy just such a limbo world, as they try to achieve an unnatural relationship, while attempting to sustain a natural one. But the limbo world of Irving's universe is more profound and frightening than that: at one point the narrator, in one of his many literary allusions, refers to Djuna Barnes's *Nightwood*, another novel about a multifaceted relationship, in which one of the characters remarks, "Man was born damned and innocent from the start, and wretchedly—as he must—on these themes—whistles his tune." Irving's character must also deal with this difficult dualism, maintaining their "weight class" in a modern world bereft of meaning and affording them no support. Writing on Barnes, Louis Kannenstine makes a point that applies equally well to Irving: "The characters, as they move between the dualities of existence, must either suffer without comprehending or collapse under an intolerable burden of understanding. The essence of the whole work, then, is enigma." Ultimately Irving, and not his narrator, suggests that the essence of his work is enigma as well—in the painting which mirrors the novel's thematic concerns, Bruegel centers a couple being led down a path by a fool, equidistant between Carnival and Lent. Irving's narrator may, in fact, be such a fool, and many of his characters do suffer without comprehending, but his more perceptive ones do not collapse. Some, like Severin Winter, learn to recognize the enigma and to grapple doggedly with its moral challenge.

JANE BOWERS HILL

John Irving's Aesthetics of Accessibility

John Irving is mad. There can be no doubt that this forty-one-year-old author of five novels, the two most recent of which spent considerable time atop best-seller lists, is not satisfied with the literary world *Time* magazine labels him a leader of. At times the anger can seem petty, even juvenile, as in William Starr's report of an April 1982 interview with Irving. Again, it can seem mystifying: exactly what is it that Irving, dissatisfied with response to his first three novels (too little public approval despite high critical praise), can complain about, having set out with *Garp* admittedly and, one presumes, *The Hotel New Hampshire* to write books that the general public would embrace, having tried and succeeded at being genuinely admired and accepted and made rich—what is it that this man has a right to be angry about?

If one carefully reads Irving's novels and criticism, and his post-*Garp* interviews, if one studies the thoughtful comments he makes about his concept of fiction in general and the novelist's job in particular, I think it is quite clear that throughout his professional life Irving has, to use one of his most common metaphors, wrestled with the problem of the fiction writer during an age when the very validity of this genre itself has been challenged. This lifelong struggle, as well as the more recently developed anger, come to full flower in Irving's 1979 essay "Kurt Vonnegut and His Critics: The

From *South Carolina Review* 16, no. 1 (Fall 1983). © 1983 by Clemson University.

Aesthetics of Accessibility." This essay makes these points: that critics have too often misread and too easily dismissed both Vonnegut's fiction and his world view precisely because Vonnegut is a popular, accessible writer: that too many contemporary writers of fiction are too busy fiddling with an elephant's left ear to notice that the elephant is standing on a baby (a metaphor Irving borrows from John Gardner); that critics, professors, and an audience primarily composed of second-year graduate students may, in fact, gravitate toward writers more difficult and obscure than Vonnegut not because their work is inherently more valuable but because their work provides more time-consuming and job-producing activities for critics, professors, and second-year graduate students; that Vonnegut's insistence, in the tradition of Shakespeare and Dickens, that art and entertainment are natural allies rather than enemies should be recognized as a strength rather than attacked as a weakness; and that what Vonnegut writes might appropriately be labeled "responsible soap opera," a label that is, for Irving, high praise.

One might at this point detail Irving's discussion of Vonnegut in order to argue for the rightness of Irving's stance about his friend, the man he calls "our strongest writer," but Irving's piece can take on objections single-handedly. What is left for discussion is the pugilistic tone of the piece and the shadowy presence of Irving's own fiction, its relation to the aesthetic theory he espouses as he defends his former teacher.

It is important, first of all, to separate Irving's call for accessible fiction from John Gardner's call for moral fiction, despite Gardner's having considered Irving one of the "up and coming moral writers." Irving parts company with Gardner over his insistence that fiction adhere to a single vision of truth, one moral in its most narrow sense; he prefers to define moral fiction as fiction that adheres to the individual writer's vision of truth, and he allows for a much broader definition of morality. Hence, a writer could, for Irving, be moral without being accessible. He does, however, support Gardner's cry for more plot and more character (in an old-fashioned sense of the words) in fiction. In addition, he sees the moral message of most broad works as "hopefully humanistic." And it is these elements—plot, character, expression of life's inherent value, along with the easily accessible quality of Vonnegut's prose—around which he chooses to shape his aesthetics of accessibility.

Historically, of course, the novel has been the accessible genre, the one born to serve the needs of a rising middle class. It was, by definition, intended for popularity. In his book, *The Early American Novel*, Henri Petter discusses what has been a catch-22 for American novelists, in particular, since the earliest days of the form in this country. Because the birth of the novel and the birth of this country are chronologically coincidental, the first American novelists attempted the almost impossible task of writing books that depended for their popularity upon responses and expectations of a not necessarily well-educated reading public, one without even the solidifying quality of a national character. Thus, the novelist was, from the beginning, faced with a choice: did he write to these expectations, whatever they might be, however faulty they might prove, and thus write books that would be read, or did he disregard these perhaps questionable expectations and fail by writing books that no one would read? Petter chronicles the decision of our earliest novelists to follow the public's expectations, a decision that led to novels often so bad that modern readers cannot get through them; certainly readers of these books have little need of the analytical skills serious readers of novels develop and rely on. One need only realize that Petter must consider Susannah Rowson's *Charlotte Temple* among the best of these books to realize how dreadfully bad the worst of them are. But Petter also sees another approach to the novelist's dilemma, one that developed fairly quickly once Americans began to write novels. He says that the best and cleverest of our early writers (Brackenridge, Brown, Washington Irving, even some of their precursors whose names are less familiar) gradually learned to use the form dictated by public expectation and thus insure an audience while they simultaneously began to expand the form, slowly and often rather clumsily bringing the American novel closer to what we might label art.

Not all novelists, however, sought to deviate from the publicly defined standards; thus, from its very beginning American fiction has been a house divided into what I will label high art and low. For purposes of quick definition, I will say that most often high art novels have fewer readers, low art novels receive less or no critical praise. In *The American Novel and Its Tradition*, Richard Chase addresses the problem of this split, first by dismissing, perhaps too easily, a 1915 Van Wyck Brooks essay which proposes that the future livelihood of the novel as a genre could best be served by a healing, a reconciliation of what Brooks calls the highbrow and lowbrow approaches. Such reconciliation would produce, according to Brooks, the most desirable course of all, the middle-brow. Chase says that such a solution, despite its "charm," would be inappropriate because it denies polarities that do exist and because it produces literature that is "generally dull and mediocre." Howells is Chase's middlebrow and, therefore, inferior novelist; his "best" writers fall into the highbrow category, James, for example, or the lowbrow, Twain, Dreiser, Norris, for instance—or into a third category Chase labels highbrow/lowbrow, a group that includes Melville, Faulkner, and Hemingway. Chase doesn't explain, but one must assume that a highbrow/lowbrow uses techniques of both schools in a purified form that preserves their integrity, while the inferior middlebrow writer somehow distills the techniques he uses so that they lose the artistic integrity that produces a "great" novel. Chase also begs the question by dealing only with novelists who are, despite where he classifies them, usually placed among the major writers of the American canon. He doesn't deal with the popular writers of best sellers. Chase does allow that this problem with middlebrow fiction is an American problem, one not shared by the British, whose fiction represents a great middlebrow tradition best represented, perhaps, by Dickens.

And Dickens is perhaps the novelist most like John Irving, the one Irving most admires. In his essay "In Defense of Sentimentality," Irving, using *A Christmas Carol* and *Great Expectations* as his examples, explains his admiration for Dickens in terms of the risks he was willing to take: "it seems that what we applaud in Dickens—his kindness, his generosity, his belief in our dignity—is also what we condemn him for (under another name) in the off-Christmas season." That other name, sentimentality, is Dickens' chief risk, is what makes him at once accessible and old-fashioned. The middlebrow, sprawling, often sentimental novels Dickens writes are not the kind of novel critics tend to praise these days; it is a strange model for a young writer coming to professional maturity in the sixties and seventies to take in order to build a reputation as a "serious" novelist. But, as Rhett Butler whispers to the widowed Scarlett O'Hara Hamilton as he sweeps her, in full mourning, onto an Atlanta dance floor, "If you have enough courage, you don't need a reputation." I think one reason Irving is so angry is that the critical world that awarded him a serious reputation on the basis of his first three novels, now calls his movement to works more overtly Dickensian in form, style, and treatment foolish or mistaken, while he sees it as courageous; but, more like Scarlett than Rhett, he wants to keep the reputation while he displays the courage.

So, Irving writes three novels, then sets out to write a novel in the manner of Dickens, one that the public would idolize in much the way they idolized, say, *A Christmas Carol* (Irving delights in Dickens' having been able to pack houses, night after night, for a reading of this book). One need only think of "The Pension Grillparzer," T. S. Garp's first significant work and of Irving's rendering of Garp's last public reading of that work to see that the comparison is not so far-fetched as it may seem if one thinks first of *Garp*'s ribaldry and sexual explicitness. Leslie Fiedler says that Irving's transition from the man who wrote *Setting Free the Bears, The Water-Method Man*, and *The 158-Pound Marriage* to the man who wrote *Garp* is an extraordinary example of a writer consciously deciding to move from high art to low, or as Fiedler perhaps more accurately labels the split, from minority writer to majority writer. Can we say then that Irving took a risk, gained popularity, lost some of his critical stature, and began to whine? Can we say that all this defense of Vonnegut and Dickens is really defense of an overly-sensitive

Irving, that his aesthetic theory is really not so much a theory as it is self-indulgence, not so much a rational effort to deal with serious questions about the nature of art as it is the easiest way to live with a self one doubts?

If we do say those things, however true they may seem, I think we too easily dismiss the important role a writer like Irving and theories such as his can play in keeping the novel alive for people, not just for critics. In *What Was Literature?* Fiedler discusses the death of the novel as an ultimate medium. He sees the high art, or minority, novel as destined for transformation into professorial notes and chalkboard diagrams and the low art, or majority, novel as created with full intention or hope of immediate translation into film. Thus, for Fiedler, the novel has already been relegated to the position of way-station, a mere pause between writer and translator, that is teacher/director. Irving's fiction stubbornly sets out to breathe new life into the genre without actually acknowledging such a death. Thus, Irving's aesthetics are not merely author as spoiled whiner, but, more importantly, author as a sort of literary lifeguard.

His methods in his own work point the way for what Irving sees as the solution to the problem of the "new" fiction, that is, the self-reflexive novel most often considered the high art novel today, the novel frequently about the novel's death that may with purpose and intention cause the very death it reflects. From his second novel, *The Water-Method Man*, through *The Hotel New Hampshire*, Irving builds into each book a character or characters who stand aghast at the new fiction: Bogus Trumper sits in the bathroom of Ralph Packer's film studio trying to read the experimental novel around which Ralph is structuring his film of Bogus' life, trying but failing; the unnamed narrator of *The 158-Pound Marriage* and his colleague/lover, Edith, are drawn together partly because of their disgust with this style of fiction, which has such a stranglehold on their academic community that the narrator's historical novels, despite respectable sales, never appear in the college's annual list of faculty publications; young Garp, afraid he doesn't understand what new fiction is about, asks Tinch, his teacher—Tinch's stuttering reply, "It's sort of fiction about fi-fi-*fiction*," reflects Irving's irritation as well as Garp's and Tinch's; and finally, John Berry, narrator of *The Hotel New Hampshire*, comes to blame new fiction, at least in part, for the suicide of his sister Lilly, the family's best-selling novelist—Lilly, having received unfavorable critical response to much of her work, finally feels she must die, being unable "to grow enough" to write the kind of book that would win the approval she needs. Irving's irony in these progressively more bitter comments on new fiction can be evaluated in terms of Lilly's small physical stature (she never reaches five feet); she feels too small, inadequate to the demands of the artistic world, but she can't be satisfied with mere popular success. She blames herself; Irving's narrator blames the world, more specifically, the world of art and criticism, for not recognizing that Lilly's soul had grown too large to fit the boundaries of the narrowly-defined genre, for which her limited stature is, of course, a metaphor.

None of these fictional characters finds an adequate solution to the questions they raise about fiction. But Irving does, a solution that brings us back to Vonnegut's responsible soap opera. Even more clearly than does Vonnegut, Irving writes just such soap opera. He says in an interview with Michael Priestly, "Most good novels are intelligent soap opera." In a post-card to his editor, the late Henry Robbins of Dutton, upon the completion of *Garp*, Irving says that book has "all the *ingredients* [my italics] of an X-rated soap opera." I emphasize the word "ingredients" because this statement is frequently misquoted or confused with one made by Garp's fictional editor, John Wolf, who said Garp's *Bensenhaver* "*is* an X-rated soap opera," Irving providing his own italics for Wolf's "is." The difference in those two state-ments is the key to the difference in what those who criticize Irving most vociferously really dislike about his work and what Irving is trying to do, which is to *use* soap opera, with all its ingredients. In other words, Irving employs the sub-genre that best embodies the popular mindset of our time, uses soap opera, as his earliest American predecessors used the grossly senti-mental, exaggerated form their public imposed upon them, to expand the boundaries of the novel to life size again, to combat the contemporary novel's anorexic tendencies. Such use of a widely accepted world view puts Irving into a tradition at least as old as Dante, whose simplicity, universality, and perpetual quality of being easy to read T. S. Eliot attributes to use of alle-gorical method, which was the common, the popular, way of looking at the universe in Dante's time. Although Eliot saw modern writers as having the problem of working in a time without a universally accepted vision of the world, Irving, writing fifty years later, seems to have solved the problem, or to have had it solved for him by a populace willing to embrace the world as soap opera. Dante was perhaps more fortunate in his audience than is Irving, but he was not any more responsible for creating it than Irving is guilty of creating his.

At the same time Irving embraces older, nineteenth-century ideas of the novel ("I am really looking upon the novel as an artform that was at its best when it was offered as a popular form. By which I probably mean the 19th-century.") and responsibly exploits the popularity of soap opera, he slips into his books, from first to last, the classic elements of modernism as defined by Monroe K. Spears: temporal, aesthetic, metaphysical, and rhetorical discontinuities. He teaches an old public (that is, a public which has, by and large, ignored new fiction) many of the tricks of that fiction. I won't enumerate specific examples, but I will note that in moving from *Setting Free the Bears* through the three middle books to *The Hotel New Hampshire*, Irving seems to be moving further from overtly including the modernist techniques and questions to more subtly acknowledging their place in the world view. Perhaps this is because he feels he can trust his readers to sense them behind his plots even as the novels move closer and closer to increasingly traditional modes of storytelling. Perhaps it is because Irving's own suspicions of modernism and new fiction have grown deeper. Whichever, Irving's interest in the role of the writer and his craft in society, as revealed in his fiction, his criticism, and his interviews, has remained strong, as strong as that of any of the writers more critically celebrated as writers of fiction about fiction.

He differs from such writers as Gass, Pynchon, Barthelme, and Barth in that his fiction about fiction insists upon the life-force of the art. Irving almost bullies his novels into life. Fiedler sees these other writers, with the exception of Barth, as content to write for each other and those professors and second-year graduate students Irving so intensely dislikes. Barth, he says, in *Letters* at least recognizes that even novels about the death of the novel are dead. But none of this, not even Barth's recognition, provides an exit from the seemingly dead-end course fiction has been set upon. Irving himself does not deny the technical brilliance such writers can attain. He tells of one of his brightest students at Iowa, a man who wrote a short story about a dinner party from the point of view of a fork; his class, with whom Irving could not disagree, considered it the best story of the semester. Its technique was brilliant, its style unmistakably modern, correct, well-executed. Irving acknowledges all this, but still he says he couldn't help actually preferring to read the long family narratives of an Indian student, narratives filled with the stumbling language of one just learning English. The Indian student's stories were also filled with people and plots and the recognition of human value. They better fit Irving's aesthetics.

Irving ends his essay on Vonnegut with a reference to Salinger's "Seymour," citing a conversation in which Seymour convinces Buddy that the chief responsibility of a writer is to his audience, even those portions of it Salinger embodies in Miss Overman, the old-maid librarian of Seymour's childhood. Irving ends another essay, one called "Trying to Save Piggy Sneed: The Making of a Writer," with a reference to his own reasons for writing fiction. He says he writes because in real life he fails to attain the level of human decency his grandmother displayed in her treatment of Piggy Sneed, the retarded garbage collector of his small-town childhood, a man who looked like, walked and talked like, the pigs he lived with, literally, and died with when his barn burned down. Irving makes up various "better" endings for Piggy Sneed, trips to Florida, Europe, language skills not retarded but refined past the comprehension of petty young boys, endings that are all lies. But the lies are necessary; they are the reasons to write as Irving writes. They are lies that make the writer and his world more decent than it is, as decent as it should be, could be. Like Vonnegut, Irving is concerned not with the elephant's left-ear hairs, but with the baby the elephant stands on, us, the world. Like Vonnegut, he wants to open that concern up to as many of us as he can, as skillfully as he can. He also, like Vonnegut, wants to entertain us. It is not my purpose to evaluate the quality of his five novels here, although, obviously, I think them very fine. It is instead my purpose to suggest that his aesthetic theory, his technique, his purpose for writing are life-affirming, that they are less concerned with ethics (Gardner's theory) or aesthetics (the theories of new fiction) than with what Fiedler calls, by way of Longinus, ecstatics; that is, Irving wants to write novels which transcend all rhetorical rules in order to dissolve the normal limits of flesh and spirit. If we allow him to do his work and he does it well, I suggest that Irving may help rescue the novel more successfully than he was able to save Piggy Sneed.

RAYMOND J. WILSON III

The Postmodern Novel: The Example of John Irving's The World According to Garp

As a novel that recapitulates within itself a history of twentieth-century fiction, John Irving's *The World According to Garp* illustrates a key aspect of postmodernism, that of formal replenishment. The earlier segments of *Garp* exhibit strong elements of modernism whereas in its final third, Irving's book is a postmodern novel of bizarre violence and black humor, flat characters, and metafiction—a mode of writing one might expect from the pen of John Barth, Robert Coover, or Thomas Pynchon. Specifically, in its first segment, *Garp* is the artist's *bildungsroman* like James Joyce's *A Portrait of the Artist as a Young Man*. Then *Garp* becomes a mid-century novel of manners dealing with the surface tone, the daily rituals, and the social patterns of American couples, its chief drama being found in adultery and sexual interaction—a novel such as one might have expected from John Updike or John Cheever. However, in John Barth's concept of a literature of exhaustion, imitation of earlier modes is a basic strategy of the post-modern novel. Thus, despite *Garp's* shifts of mode, as a contemporary fiction operating in three modes, it must be intrinsically postmodern throughout. My analysis proceeds in two stages: first, a theoretical overview of postmodernism, followed by the specific example of *The World According to Garp*.

From *Critique: Studies in Modern Fiction* 34, no. 1 (Fall 1992). © 1992 by the Helen Dwight Reid Educational Foundation.

Postmodern Fiction

The term *postmodern* requires careful investigation. Since the 1960s, readers have noticed a difference in some of our fiction; attempting to discuss this new fiction without long circumlocutions, critics invented a term: *postmodern fiction*. Attempts to define this expression followed its use but led to a problem. As John Barth points out, no agreement has been reached on a definition; and because widespread agreement has not yet been reached even for a definition of modernism, we cannot expect a rapid agreement of a definition of postmodernism. In this situation we might find it effective not to attempt a strict logical definition but simply to list those characteristics that first made us notice a difference. In this essay, I suggest a noninclusive list: (1) a propensity to contain and reuse all previous forms in a literature of exhaustion and replenishment; (2) a zone of the bizarre, where fantasy best expresses our sense of reality; (3) a turning away from penetration into the psychological depth of character as the primary goal of fiction; and (4) a propensity for metafiction, in which writing draws attention to the techniques and processes of its own creation.

A literature of exhaustion and replenishment

The postmodern novel contains all the earlier modes of the novel, contains them intrinsically within the process by which a literature of exhausted possibilities replenishes itself. Such commentators as Albert J. La Valley, Herman Kahn, and Christopher Lasch may see causes of change in recent literature in deep cultural contexts. La Valley says that the new literature reflects a new consciousness that has been "inspired in part by the breakdown of our culture, its traditions, and its justifications of the American social structure"; Kahn and Wiener refer to our culture as being in the "Late Sensate" stage, our art, including literature, reflecting a culture in the state of decline; and Lasch argues that "Bourgeois society seems everywhere to have used up its store of constructive ideas" and that there is "a pervasive despair of understanding the course of modern history or of subjecting it to rational direction." However, the originator of the expression "literature of exhaustion," John Barth, referred to it as "the literature of exhausted possibilities" and says that by "'exhaustion' I don't mean anything so tired as the subject of physical, moral or intellectual decadence, only the usedupness of certain forms or exhaustion of certain possibilities." Despair might be the reaction of a contemporary writer of fiction when he or she faces the realization that the limited number of possible variations in the form of fiction may have already been explored, but Barth has an answer. While today's author may panic at the idea of being condemned to merely repeat what a Flaubert, a James, a Fitzgerald, or a Joyce has discovered and what countless others have already repeated, Barth finds the situation "by no means necessarily a cause for despair."

The escape from panic, Barth finds, comes in a story by Borges. In the story "Pierre Menard, Author of *Quixote*," Borges described his character Menard's astonishing effort of will in producing—composing, not copying—several chapters of Cervantes' *Don Quixote*. Borges's narrator points out that despite being verbally identical the recomposition is a new, fresh work: what for Cervantes was merely an everyday, workmanlike style of prose is for Menard a clever, playful use of quaint, semi-antiquated diction; what for Cervantes were mere commonplaces of conventional rhetoric can be for Menard a series of radical, exciting departures from the accepted wisdom of his day. Barth points out that it would have "been sufficient for Menard to have *attributed* the novel to himself in order to have a new work of art, from the intellectual point of view." However, Barth feels that "the important thing to observe is that Borges *doesn't* attribute the *Quixote* to himself, much less recompose it like Pierre Menard; instead, he writes a remarkable and original work of literature, the implicit theme of which is the difficulty, perhaps the unnecessity, of writing original works of literature. Barth believes that Borges's "artistic victory," emerges from confronting "an intellectual dead end," and employing it "against itself to accomplish new human work."

In its reuse of earlier forms, we can see how *The World According to Garp* is related to postmodern works by John Barth and Robert Coover. In "Menelaiad," a story in *Lost in the Funhouse*, John Barth parodies the Greek epic form; and in *The Sot-Weed Factor*, Barth contorts the genre of the eighteenth-century novel. It would be a mistake to think that Barth is writing an epic or an eighteenth-century novel. Nor is Barth really writing a Richardsonian epistolary novel in *Letters*. Instead, Barth writes a postmodern novel that plays with the form. Similarly, Coover is not writing a mystery in *Gerald's Party*; instead, this novel, as William Gass is quoted as saying on the dust jacket, "sends up the salon mystery so far it will never come down. What comes down is a terrible indictment of our desires." Just so, *The World According to Garp* plays with the modernist forms of the artist's *bildungsroman* and the midcentury American comedy of manners and necessarily makes an implicit comment upon them, as I shall argue later. *Garp*, by its reuse of modernist forms, stands in the same territory as these works by Barth and Coover.

By reusing existing forms this new fiction opens for itself doors to endless opportunities for freshness. Borges's story, for example, is itself a parody of the critical article. The postmodern novel's parody reveals a literary form returning to its point of origin to renew itself. Barth points out that the *Quixote* is itself a parody of an earlier form—the poetic romance. One thinks immediately of Defoe's stories parodying news articles and his novels in the form of personal reminiscences. Richardson is said to have begun *Pamela* as a model set of letters for young ladies and to have thus invented the English epistolary novel almost by accident.

The zone of the bizarre

Because the term *zone* comes from *Gravity's Rainbow*, this category highlights the relationship between *Garp* and Thomas Pynchon's great novel. Speaking of the zone of occupation in defeated Germany, Brian McHale says that as *Gravity's Rainbow* unfolds, "hallucinations and fantasies become real, metaphors become literal, the fictional worlds of the mass media—the movies, comic-books—thrust themselves into the midst of historical reality." As such, "Pynchon's zone is paradigmatic for the heterotopian space of post-modernist writing." *The World According to Garp* has a zone, as I shall argue, that fits *Gravity's Rainbow*'s paradigm. Brian McHale suggests that behind all the postmodernist fictional construction of zones "lies Apollinaire's poem, 'Zone' (from *Alcools*, 1913), whose speaker, strolling through the immigrant and red-light districts of Paris, finds in them an objective correlative for modern Europe and his own marginal, heterogeneous, and outlaw experience." However, an even better explanation might be found in Philip Roth's observation that "the toughest problem for the American writer was that the substance of the American experience itself was so abnormally and fantastically strange, it had become an 'embarrassment to one's own meager imagination.'" "If reality becomes surrealistic," Joe David Bellamy asks, "what must fiction do to be realistic?" It must become bizarre, goes one answer.

The bizarre connects realistic fiction to fantasy and myth. Fantasy is an old form that takes on new implications when used consciously by the contemporary writer, not as an alternative or escape from reality but as the best method available for catching the emotional essence of our era. The distinction between fantasy and myth is not always easy to maintain when one looks at individual stories, although theoretically a mythically structured story may maintain a surface sense of realism the way a fantasy story cannot.

Also connected to the bizarre characteristic of these zones is the post-modern novel's black humor. In *The Fabulators*, Robert Scholes says that black humorists, in a century of historical horror, deal with the absurdity of "the human situation" by seeing it "as a cosmic joke." He suggests that in contrast to the existentialist, the black humorist offers an alternative: "The best response is neither acquiescence nor bitterness"; rather one must play "one's role in the joke in such a way as to turn the humor back on the joker or cause it to diffuse itself harmlessly on the whole group which has participated in the process of the joke."

As the extreme epitome of the atmosphere of much postmodern fiction, the zone of the bizarre compensates for its retreat from the strict tenets of realism by evoking echoes of no-less-real feelings from our personas pasts, feelings that today we can experience only in dreams or in moments of great stress—of terror, perhaps—when our "normal" functioning breaks down. Although we repress these feelings, we react with a mixture of anxiety and secret welcoming when the television news reports events that cannot be grasped without reference to such emotions. Through the bizarre, postmodern fiction taps and reflects this source of emotional power and does so, not despite, but because of its departure from the formal tenets of "realism," which center on an attempt to penetrate into the depths of character.

Umberto Eco notes the shift in contemporary novels, where an author "renounces all psychology as the motive of narrative and decides to transfer characters and situations to the level of an objective structural strategy." Eco sees this "choice familiar to many contemporary disciplines" as one in which an author passes "from the psychological method to the formalistic one." Eco's words fit with Robert Scholes's prediction that the key element in the coming new fiction would be a new dimension of the "care for form." This noncharacter orientation provides a point of reference between *The World According to Garp* and Robert Coover's *The Universal Baseball Association*, which is organized neither by plot nor by revelation of its intentionally flat characters but by the structural relationship of game and ritual and the progressive transformation of the one into the other.

Metafiction

Metafiction is another instance where fiction turns away from outside reality and seeks a subject intrinsically suited to the written word. In this method, the technique of composition becomes to some extent the subject of fiction itself. If television and movies are vastly better adapted to creating an illusion of reality—the depiction of objects—then fiction must find other subjects for its own survival, just as painting turned to the nonrepresentational when painters recognized the photograph's power to recreate a scene accurately. In the metafictional dimension, we see the connection of *The World According to Garp* to other postmodern fiction, for example to the stories of John Barth's

Lost in the Funhouse, especially the title story, in which the implied author presents himself as trying—and failing—to write a conventional story by the cookbook-recipe method but actually writing a postmodern story. Of another story in the volume, "Autobiography," Barth says in his author's note, that it is "the story, speaking of itself."

THE WORLD ACCORDING TO GARP AS POSTMODERN FICTION

Reuse of earlier forms

As a novel that shifts from mode to mode, *The World According to Garp* illustrates the postmodern as a literature of replenishment: *Garp* recapitulates within itself a history of the twentieth-century novel, performing a tacit critique of the earlier forms. Irving starts in an early twentieth-century mode. Reviewing the fiction of this era, Irving Howe says that whereas nineteenth-century realism studied social classes, early twentieth-century fiction studied the rebellion of the Stephen Dedaluses against behavior patterns imposed by social classes in a particular country. In this conception, the modern novel came into being when James Joyce reconstructed the existing form of the *bildungsroman* to create *A Portrait*. More than merely recasting the autobiographical novel into the "individuating rhythm" of *Dubliners*, Joyce helped form the modern consciousness itself. D. H. Lawrence's *Sons and Lovers* shares this feature with Joyce's *A Portrait*; and although Lawrence's novel retains more of the trappings of nineteenth-century realism than Joyce's book, both create characters that do not fit into their own world but who express an aesthetic that is familiar in our intellectual climate. John Irving achieves similar effects in his *bildungsroman*.

The *bildungsroman* form is suited to linearity of narrative flow, reflecting the linear growth of a boy's life. In the McCaffery interview, John Irving claimed that he was "very conscious of attempting to make my narrative as absolutely linear as possible. . . . With my first four novels I was always troubled," says Irving, "particularly with *Garp*, about the convoluted flow of my narrative. . . . *Garp* was, in fact, a kind of minor breakthrough for me just in the sense that it was the first novel I managed to order chronologically." Irving rejects the unreadable masterpieces of high modernist literature and implies that he is returning to the simpler forms of earlier days; however, no nineteenth-century author could have written *The World According to Garp*. John Irving is moving on into postmodernism, as the three-segment analysis of the novel can demonstrate.

As in the early works of Joyce and Lawrence, the opening section of

Garp fits the genre's depiction of parents and childhood surroundings. In the chapter entitled "Blood and Blue," Garp's near fall from a roof and his being bitten by a dog parallel Stephen Dedalus's being shouldered into a playground puddle and having his hands smacked by his teacher. And similarly, the succeeding chapters fulfill other criteria for the genre, combining Garp's sexual initiation with an encounter with pain and death in the demise of the prostitute named Charlotte.

Garp's involvement with the death of this "whore," whom he had come to know better than Joyce's Stephen knew the prostitutes he visited, precipitates Garp's forming his working aesthetic as a writer. Combined with the play of Garp's imagination on the war damage at the Vienna zoo, the death of Charlotte ties Garp's emergence as an adult to his emergence as a writer: a creator and reflector of modern consciousness like Stephen Dedalus. Garp had been unable to finish the story that would make him a "real writer." "The Pension Grillparzer," as the story was called, consisted of two major elements that Garp was having trouble reconciling: a continuous line of hilarious, almost farcical action, low comedy, approaching slapstick that coexisted with a somber theme generated by a dream-omen of death. After Charlotte's death, Garp fell under "a writer's long-sought trance, wherein the world falls under one embracing tone of voice." Here, Irving's narrator emphasizes the importance of what Gerard Genette, following Tzvetan Todorov, has called "aspect," or "the way in which the story is perceived by the narrator."

Visiting the zoo that still bore the signs of war damage, "Garp discovered that when you are writing something, everything seems related to everything else." In the evidences of war Garp saw the connection between larger human history and each person's individual history and so was able to finish the story. His notion of modern consciousness is that "the history of a city was like the history of a family—there is a closeness, and even affection, but death eventually separates everyone from each other." It may be that this is an aesthetic as appropriate for the post-Hiroshima era as Stephen Dedalus's aesthetic was for the era he heralded. Finishing the story after having formed his guiding aesthetic, Garp met Helen's standard for a "real" writer and thus "earned" a wife for himself. Thus, Irving completed the segment of the novel with the forecast that "in their stubborn, deliberate ways," Helen and Garp would fall in love with each other "sometime after they had married."

Irving's implicit comment on the Joycean *bildungsroman* is ironic. By writing in the form, Irving is affirming the value of the early modernist mode, despite his rejection of excessively complicated modernist literature in the McCaffery interview. However, even an affirmation is a comment, and a comment on modernism is not modernism; by its nature, a comment of modernism must be something standing outside of modernism, viewing it, and implicitly judging it. The existence of bizarre violence and the associated vein of black humor, even in the first section of the book, contributes to irony. The novel opens to the backdrop of a war, and Jenny Fields's brusque categorizing of the wounded into classes of Externals, Vital Organs, Absentees, and Goners certainly contains an element of the blackly humorous. In its vividness, Jenny's slashing of a persistent masher verges on the gothic. Garp's being bitten by a dog is merely an element of *bildungsroman*, but Garp's biting off the ear of the dog verges on the bizarre. With their hint of anti-realist absurdism, these elements provide a counterpoint to the modernist mode, repeatedly rupturing it, threatening to radicalize the novel into the postmodern, and foreshadowing the third section where the transformation does occur. Implicit in these ruptures is the notion that the early modernist mode has difficulty expressing a contemporary reality that itself has become postmodern.

A similar point and counterpoint arises in the second section of the novel. Here, John Irving introduces a mid-century novel of manners, a section of *Garp* that approximates the aura of an Updike novel or a Cheever story. The central characteristic of the cultural attitude found in mid-century can be illuminated by an insight Stanley Kaufmann drew from the words of a contemporary Italian filmmaker: "When Vittorio de Sica was asked why so many of his films deal with adultery, he is said to have replied, 'But if you take adultery out of the lives of the bourgeoisie, what drama is left?'" The middle segment of Irving's novel, which culminates with Garp's discovery of Helen's affair with Michael Milton, contains the tale of a suburban marriage, its fidelities and infidelities: Garp's sexual encounter with a babysitter, his resisting an attempted seduction by "Mrs. Ralph," and a temporary swap of sexual partners between the Garps and a couple named Harry and Alice—a situation like that with which Updike dealt in his novel *Couples*.

The suburban domestic tale fits Howe's belief that mid-century fiction, having abandoned the rebellious stance of a Stephen Dedalus, studied the search for values (looking for them, to some degree, in marriage) by a people who live in a world where social class may still exist but where it no longer dominates every detail of daily existence or predestines one to as limited a range of expectations as did the earlier class system. Fitting with Howe's analysis, the point of reference in the middle of *Garp*, as in the mainstream American novel in the middle of the century, is sociological; the question asked is whether monogamous marriage, as it is found in suburbia, can sustain or bring happiness to people of any sensitivity. What Garp said about his second novel might describe both the midsection of *Garp* and the American novel at mid-century: it was "a serious comedy about marriage," Garp said, "but a sexual farce."

The central section is made ironic by isolated outcroppings of the bizarre, which implicitly undermine our belief in the fruitfulness of this modernist form. The marriage-comedy/sex-farce enclosed an episode in which Garp helps in the capture of a man who habitually rapes little girls, a sequence that takes on ominous implications when Garp happens to meet the rapist who has been released on a legal technicality, collecting tickets at a basketball game. Implicit in the counterpoint created by the intrusion of public and epochal violence into the private and personal is the conclusion that a mode, such as mid-century modernist realism, the Updike/Cheever comedy of manners, which exists to reveal the private and personal, loses its force.

The reader can guess at the historical moment recreated in Irving's implicit irony from a comment Saul Bellow made about novelists of the early 1960s who sought to "examine the private life." Bellow says that some "cannot find the [private] life they are going to examine. The power of public life has become so vast and threatening that private life cannot maintain a pretense of its importance." Unhappy with the situation in which modernist fiction found itself, some authors began turning away, as Irving Howe has noted, from "realistic portraiture" to express their spirit in "fable, picaresque, prophecy, and nostalgia." Novels by these writers, Howe says, "constitute what I would class 'post-modern fiction.'" Howe was identifying a trend that came to be designated, much more inclusively, by the term he used in 1959.

We are deeply involved in the serio-comic complications of Garp's marriage-comedy/sex-farce when an auto accident wrenches us into the postmodern mode—the accident that killed one of Garp's little boys and maimed the other. The transfer between modes comes from a shattering experience—the accident and its physical and emotional consequences. An analogy (with an important difference) can be seen in the work of Saul Bellow. Irving Howe says that when Bellow writes in *Henderson the Rain King*, "that men need a shattering experience to 'wake the spirit's sleep,' we soon realize that his ultimate reference is to America, where many spirits sleep." Bellow, though he keeps his mode in the realistic mainstream, takes his character to Africa for the shattering experience; Irving keeps the scene in America, but this America has become a postmodern "zone" and is no longer the familiar scene of an Updike novel.

The zone of the bizarre

The nearly gothic episodes of the first two sections prepare us for the novel's final section. The salient events in the third section are intrusions of public life into the private: assassinations, mob violence, and highway mayhem, much of it not accidental. The public/private dichotomy presents itself most clearly in Garp's refusal to accept the fact that a strictly women's memorial service for his mother, Jenny Fields, is not a private funeral but a public, political event. It would be unthinkable to bar a son from the one, but unthinkable to welcome a man to the other.

As for the bizarre, not only is the setting moved to Jenny Field's madcap home for "injured women" at Don's Head Harbor; but even more significantly, we suddenly find ourselves in a world as strange as the fictional zones of a Thomas Pynchon or a John Hawkes, if not one reaching the extremes of a William Burroughs. In the final section of Irving's novel, T. S. Garp expresses the dominant feeling: "*Life* is an X-rated soap opera." Akin to both fantasy and myth, this feeling becomes progressively objectified when the horrible "Under Toad" first grows from a family joke, introduced analeptically, into a code word for speaking about a hovering fear. Then, although the reader's mind tries to reject overt supernaturalism, the Under Toad becomes a veritable character, a vengeful beast who at times becomes as real as Grendel in the Old English poem. The myth-fantasy dimension of Irving's novel would thus partake of what Tzvetan Todorov calls "the fantastic"; in the book of that name, Todorov defines the state as a hovering between "the uncanny," in which apparently supernatural events receive some ultimate natural explanation, and "the marvelous," in which the supernatural becomes the norm. McHale finds such "hesitation" to be characteristic of postmodernist fiction.

Significantly, the Under Toad is mentioned only in the third section of the book, although its origin—in a little boy's misunderstanding of his father's warning about the "undertow" on the beach—occurs in the chronological middle of the book. There may be technical reasons why Irving decided to develop the Under Toad only in retrospect, after the reader knows of little Walt's death. Even so, it is clear that the fantasy and myth aspects of the Under Toad contribute to a mode of postmodernism in the novel's concluding section, reminding us for example of Pynchon's notion that the modern world can only be fathomed through the agency of paranoia. The Under Toad's myth and fantasy elements would have been less appropriate in the more realistic, comic-farce mode of *Garp*'s center section, but they provide an ideal backdrop for black humor.

Garp's death itself typifies black humor "in its random, stupid, and unnecessary qualities—comic and ugly and bizarre" in the words of the novel itself. "In the world according to Garp," the novel says, "an evening could be hilarious and the next morning could be murderous." These elements of the bizarre, myth/fantasy, and black humor distract the reader from a feature that arouses curiosity when first noticed, that the characters have flattened out.

Flatness of character

The third section, more than the first two, bears out the postmodern ethic by which to declare a character psychologically flat need not be to denigrate the author's skill. Irving's mistrust of over psychologizing may have led to his statement that "the phrase 'psychologically deep' is a contradiction of terms." Irving feels that such a view "is a terribly simplistic and unimaginative approach. Ultimately it is destructive of all the breadth and complexity in literature." Complexity in the final third of *Garp* arises from structure, from ironic genre manipulation, from the problematic nature of the text's relationship to the world, and not from any probing of psychological motive that might lead to internal character revelation. The third section of the text is marked by a lack of interest in motive: of assassins, of the Ellen Jamesians, of Garp when he insists on performing actions that he knows draw destruction down upon himself, even though he desires safety. While reflecting the postmodern distrust of "the subject" as a useful category, the flattening of character in the third section of *Garp* may, even more, express a sense of the individual's powerlessness within an absurd situation.

The novel draws its unity, not from continuity of plot, as in the premodernist novel, nor from analysis of character, a feature of modernist fiction, but partially from the operation of motif: a repetition of impaired speech that interacts with a counter-motif of "writing." Garp's father had a speech impediment stemming from profound brain damage suffered in war. From then on, the novel contains numerous other instances of impaired speech, depicted either as a temporary or a permanent condition. Apparently permanently afflicted are Alice Hindman, whose speech problem is a psychological outgrowth of her marriage problems; Ellen James, who was raped and left tongueless by men who did not have the sense to realize that she was old enough to implicate them by writing; the Ellen Jamesians, women who have their tongues removed in sympathy with Ellen; and Garp's high school English teacher Tinch and Tinch's eventual replacement, Donald Whitcomb who was to become Garp's biographer. Temporarily "struck dumb" were the young girl whose rapist Garp had helped capture, and Garp himself—for a long while after his auto accident and for the few moments he lived after being shot by Pooh Percy. Pooh's rage, her inarticulate curses from a gaping self-wounded mouth, forms a near-tableau at the end of Garp's life to match the one at its beginning when his future father's decreasing level of articulation from "Garp" to "Arp" to "Ar" led Jenny to realize that he was soon to die and spurred her to get on with the business of Garp's conception. In between, Garp was to wonder "Why is my life so full of people with impaired speech?" He then asks, "Or is it only because I'm a writer that I notice all the damaged voices around me?"

Compensating for the flatness of character, providing coherence within the zone of the bizarre, these repeated elements are the motor oil for the postmodern fictional machine. Their theme of speech brings us to the author's means of speaking to us, his fiction. Having made ironic modernist realism's implicit claim to tell us about the world, the postmodern fictionist has questioned the writer's own instrument, and he or she thus often turns to examine it in the reader's presence. Irving is not exempt from this tendency toward metafiction.

Metafiction

Irving's novel alludes to the phenomenon of metafiction when discussing the rejection note that Garp received for "The Pension Grillparzer": *"The story is only mildly interesting, and it does nothing new with language or with form."* Tinch, Garp's former instructor, said he really did not understand the "newer fiction" except that it was supposed to be "about it-it-itself. . . . It's sort of fiction about fi-fi-*fic*tion," Tinch told Garp. Garp did not understand either and, in truth, cared mainly about the fact that Helen liked the story. But although Garp was not interested in metafiction at this stage of his career, we can see that Irving is to some degree practicing this aspect of the new fiction in the third section of *Garp*. While the accounts of Garp's earlier novels may bear a certain resemblance to Irving's own earlier works, these need not be considered metafictional manifestations; one merely suspects Irving of a certain wry humor of self parody, while he remains in the traditional mode of autobiographical fiction or even within the mere technique of an author drawing on his own experience for his fiction. In contrast, when we enter the third section we encounter Garp's novel *The World According to Bensenhaver*, with its obvious similarity in title to *The World According to Garp*. Although there are significant differences between the novel we are reading and the one we are reading about, the parallels and even the comedy of the differences cannot help but act as implicit comments upon the technique and compositional process of *Garp*.

"'Life,' Garp wrote," according to the novel, "'is sadly *not* structured like a good old-fashioned novel. Instead, an ending occurs where those who are meant to peter out have petered out.'" Such a metafictional comment in the third section does not surprise us. Indeed, we see this mode occurring repeatedly. When Garp's publisher, John Wolf, was dying he asked Garp's son Duncan "What would your father say to this? . . . Wouldn't it suit one of *his* death scenes? Isn't it properly grotesque?" To the extent that we could ask this question equally of Irving as of Garp, the question has metafictional implications, as does what Wolf said about Garp's own grotesque mode of dying: "It was a death scene, John Wolf told Jillsy Sloper, that only Garp could have written." When a character in a novel says that a death scene in that novel occurred in a way which "only" the dying character could have written, we are involved with metafiction.

The structure of the final chapter, which opens with a comment on Garp's fictional technique, has further metafictional implications: "He loved epilogues, as he showed us in 'The Pension Grillparzer.' 'An epilogue,' Garp wrote 'is more than a body count. An epilogue, in the disguise of wrapping up the past, is really a way of warning us about the future.'" And the final chapter—the nineteenth, identical to the number of chapters in *The World According to Bensenhaver*—ends with just such an epilogue. Irving's narrator makes the metafictional element nearly explicit: "He would have liked the idea of an epilogue, too," says the narrator after Garp's death, "—so here it is: an epilogue 'warning us about the future,' as T. S. Garp might have imagined it." Thus the final twenty pages of the novel present us the interesting metafictional situation of an author writing the epilogue to his character's death as the narrator says the character would himself have imagined it. Metafiction, combined with the zone of the bizarre and the turn away from psychological depth makes the third section of the novel postmodern. While the first two thirds exhibit far less of these characteristics and more of those of earlier modes, these sections exhibit the postmodern reuse of earlier forms; thus, *Garp* is postmodern throughout.

In writing this novel, Irving stays true to his rejecting the spirit of the unreadable masterpieces of high modernism, but he is not returning to the mode of the nineteenth century; he is moving forward into postmodernism. In his desire to avoid the esoteric, Irving might find an ally in John Barth, who in "The Literature of Replenishment: Postmodernist Fiction" offers his "worthy program" in hopes that the postmodern mode may become a fiction "more democratic in its appeal" than the marvels of late modernism, reaching beyond the "professional devotees of high art" but perhaps not hoping to reach the "lobotomized mass-media illiterates." In its best-seller popularity, *The World According to Garp* has at least fulfilled that aspect of Barth's program for postmodern fiction. This success may be described by the proposition that the postmodern novel, besides its special characteristics, also contains all earlier fictional forms, and John Irving's use of two of them opens his novel to a fruitful variety of combination and interaction.

DEBRA SHOSTAK

The Family Romances of John Irving

John Irving's *The Hotel New Hampshire* (1981) begins with a story-telling father, telling "Father's story." He is the origin of story and the origin of the children who will populate the story, and his word is intimately known: "That was the line Father usually began with—the line he began with the first time I remember being told the story." While this opening is self-conscious in its reference to how stories are told, it is also unself-conscious in its sentimental deference to the father, the familial authority—an upper-case Father—who remains nameless for several pages because, the narrator assumes, he is already as well known as his stories and his authorship is unimpeachable. I suggest that there exists an important link between the two seemingly unrelated predilections illustrated here—the focus on fathers, present and absent, and the inclination toward self-conscious form—perhaps best explained in terms of the "family romance." This Freudian plot of psychological development describes in particular the boy's fantasy of replacing his parents with others of higher social standing, and his subsequent recognition that, while one's biological mother can be established, one's father is always uncertain; according to Freud, the boy's fantasies become erotic, as he imagines the "secret love-affairs" in which his mother might have engaged in order to conceive him or his siblings. The latter phase, of course, represents just one feature of Freud's formulation concerning the filial relationship, the Oedipus complex. Because that relation-

From *Essays in Literature* 21, no. 1 (Spring 1994). © 1994 by Western Illinois University.

ship, as Harold Bloom has argued, can stand as a compelling analogy for the relationship between a writer and his (rarely her) precursors, the figure of the family romance illuminates some of the central questions of Irving's fiction. Those questions, existing simultaneously at textual and extratextual levels, concern paternity and paternal authority: Who is the father? Where lies the source of psychological and, more specifically, aesthetic identity? How do texts derive from their origins? Because Irving's answers tend to be contradictory, his fiction provides a useful field on which to explore oedipal conflicts.

The first conflict emerges when one compares Irving's representational modes to his descriptions of his fictional values: specifically, his simultaneous use and stated abhorrence of metafictional techniques. According to Patricia Waugh's concise description, metafiction explores "the function of language in constructing and maintaining our sense of everyday 'reality,'" wherein language is seen as "an independent, self-contained system which generates its own 'meanings.'" Perhaps the most obvious example of metafiction among Irving's novels appears in *The World According to Garp* (1978), which features a self-reflexive structure, interpolating Garp's fiction into the narrative of Garp's life as a way of commenting on the relationship between a lived reality and the making of art. Central to the inquiry posed by *Garp*'s embedded stories is a question that Waugh finds metafiction repeatedly asking about frames: "What is the 'frame' that separates reality from 'fiction'?". *Garp* first announces its metafictional dimension in the "according" of the title, which asks readers to accept the authority of Garp's voice in writing his fiction even as it undermines that authority by pointing out its perspectival nature. For the self-conscious red herring of the title reminds us that there is another voice framing Garp's, a ventriloquist of an author who is the actual authority over the "reality" of Garp's life and the writing of his fiction.

Evidence of Irving's metafictional proclivities exists in most of his other novels as well. *Setting Free the Bears* (1968) has a tripartite structure whose centerpiece, "The Notebook," interleaves Siggy Javotnik's observation reports at the Hietzinger zoo with short chapters from his "highly selective autobiography," a "pre-history" that tells the story of his parents before his birth. This structural complexity, which embeds two stages of Siggy's history within an account of the current actions of the narrator, Hannes Graff, makes a comment on the way stories of the past and events of the present create meaning reciprocally. Irving's second novel, *The Water-Method Man* (1972), has a self-remarking, convoluted structure as well. The novel's rapid shifts between times, places, and narrative points of view imitate the central metaphor of the novel, Bogus Trumper's "narrow, winding road" of a urinary tract, which, in turn, stands for the evasions and repressions in his life. The numerous references to devising linear texts—making films, or say, writing dissertations—ironize the unconscious motivations in Trumper's rambling creation of his life's narrative. *The Hotel New Hampshire* experiments with casting the family saga in the form of a fairy tale which, in focusing on the children's travails in growing up, accommodates a generically idealized "Mother" and "Father" as well as brutality, grotesquerie, and a woman who denies her identity by living in a bear suit. The novel is a fairy tale that serves to question its own form, showing how the conventions of fable may account or fail to account for the everyday reality of a contemporary American family. Even the third novel, *The 158-Pound Marriage* (1973), in some ways more linear in its narrative than its precursors, nevertheless includes stories within stories and provides a comment on its own fictionality in its structural allusions—by way of its sexual ménage between two couples—to Ford Madox Ford's *The Good Soldier* and John Hawkes's *The Blood Oranges*.

But perhaps the most obvious sign of Irving's fictional self-reflexiveness is that every one of his seven novels includes within it at least one character who writes, whose writing is reproduced or at least described within the text, and in whose writing one can discern attempts to construct a linguistic "reality" that may or may not accord with the "reality" represented in the frame narrative. Graff arranges Siggy's journals and autobiography in *Setting Free the Bears* by conscious design. In *The Water-Method Man*, Trumper, who invents and embellishes rather than simply translating the "Old Low Norse" poem that is the subject of his dissertation, keeps a diary which turns out to be the novel we are reading. Here, too, the act of writing in its function to create experience is consistently underscored by Irving's inclusion of letters, stories, and snippets of Trumper's Old Low Norse poem within the texture of the novel. *The 158-Pound Marriage* is narrated by a man whose insensitivity to events around him assures us not only that the historical novels he writes lack perceptiveness but that he is deeply invested in using his narration to repress and reinvent his reality. His opposite number and partner in the mate-swapping plot is a woman novelist whose scripting of their affair, unsuspected by him, and whose more imaginatively successful work likewise reveal a desire to construct a reality. Not only is Garp a writer of fiction, but his mother, Jenny Fields, gains vast fame—not to mention an assassin—for writing her autobiography, *A Sexual Suspect*. In newly identifying the constraints under which she has operated as a mid-century American woman, her narrative rewrites popular knowledge about the social construction of identity such that Jenny becomes the leader of a national movement.

Among the less formal or public writers of the later novels, the narrator in *The Hotel New Hampshire* announces that he is the family member who, because "the middle child, and the least opinionated," must "set the record straight" about the family's story; part of the story he "writes" in his narration is about the early success and suicide of his young sister, who has written a memoir about growing up. Irving permits a level of irony in relation to the narrator, whose apparently naive stance and lack of "opinion," we come to realize, are nevertheless colored by his incestuous feelings for another sister. Wilbur Larch, venerable doctor and director of the orphanage at the center of *The Cider House Rules* (1985), keeps a comprehensive journal, frequently "quoted" in the text, which includes a history of the town, a record of daily activities, and his obsessive musings about his favorite orphan, the novel's protagonist, Homer Wells. The last, overtly subjective, focus presents an increasingly ironic counterpoint to the seemingly more objective passages of history, as Larch begins to invent a "history" for Homer. The imaginative flights of this biography may be seen to undermine Larch's authority as historian in the other passages of his journal. Finally, *A Prayer for Owen Meany* (1989) includes another diarist, Owen Meany, and a hagiographer of sorts—John Wheelwright, who narrates Owen's story, and whose construction of that story is clearly influenced by his conclusions about Owen's final "meaning." In each case, then, Irving draws attention to the act of writing as it constructs both the realities in which the characters participate and the "reality" of the narratives we read.

While Irving's last two books, *The Cider House Rules* and *A Prayer for Owen Meany*, attempt to resist fictional self-consciousness, especially in their use of linear structure, both novels include references on the part of their narrators to how the narratives take their shape as well as self-references to Irving's other books—to cite only one example, the passing allusion in *The Cider House Rules* to "lunacy and sorrow," a line conspicuously featured in *The World According to Garp*. Yet despite the fiction's reflexive play, Irving has indicated his opposition to the implicit philosophies and narrative modes of metafiction. Most obvious are the digs that appear in the novels themselves. Both *The Water-Method Man* and *The 158-Pound Marriage* satirize a writer of the "new novel" named Helmbart, a virtual anagram for the names of two prominent metafictionists, John Barth and Donald Barthelme. In *The 158-Pound Marriage*, Helmbart turns up as a despicable lecher; two characters agree about his writing that "when the subject of fiction became how to write fiction, we lost interest; we were interested in prose, surely, but not when the subject of the prose became prose itself." He appears earlier in *The Water-Method Man* as the author of "a contemporary novel" titled *Vital Telegrams*. Bogus Trumper reads a chapter of it, which Irving "reproduces" in his text; the chapter is a chaotic collection of pretentious fragments of plot, which Trumper judges unreadable. In these pointed allusions, Irving seems to characterize metafiction, which tends to foreground its own technique, as incoherent, unfelt, and intellectually obscure.

He has also in his own persona divorced himself from such writing. "I'm not a twentieth-century novelist, I'm not modern, and certainly not postmodern," he told Ron Hansen. He tends to use words like "literary" pejoratively, making a distinction between "real writers" and "academic" writers and retrospectively disdaining the structural convolutions of a novel like *The Water-Method Man* as "showing off." In his essay "Kurt Vonnegut and His Critics," Irving disparages those writers—mostly unnamed, but clearly associated with metafiction—who prize an aesthetic of difficulty or obscurity, and he instead praises the old-fashioned virtues of readability, entertainment, and catharsis. Here he works to expose as false the assumption "that what is easy to read has been easy to write" and argues that clarity and depth of ideas are not mutually exclusive. Irving repeatedly insists that art must entertain, and that to be entertaining it must be accessible; he implies that the technical display of the "new novel" is anything but entertaining or accessible.

Irving's remedy for the illnesses of complexity and self-flaunting or hermetic technique is his return increasingly in his novels to the conventions of Victorian fiction. He remarked in 1986 that "I follow the form of the nineteenth-century novel. . . . I'm old-fashioned, a storyteller. I'm not an analyst and I'm not an intellectual." The mode is comic realism, the material is what he terms "intelligent soap opera," and the master is Charles Dickens. When Irving claims that "Entertainment is one of the many *aesthetic* obligations of art," the first examples he names are Shakespeare and Dickens. He describes *Great Expectations* as a soap opera, "given dignity by how well [it's] done." Irving praises Dickens's courage in risking sentimentality in order to write books that will matter emotionally, and he cites George Santayana in arguing that what readers may dismiss as exageration or sentimentality in Dickens is in fact his exposure of what we really are ("In Defense of Sentimentality"). Irving's debt to Dickens is repaid in a variety of ways—the bizarre or eccentric characters who populate his fictional terrain, the comic names, the homage in *The Cider House Rules* by way of numerous allusions to *David Copperfield* and *Great Expectations*, which are bibles to the orphan Homer Wells. But Dickens's influence is most pervasive in the scope of Irving's canvases, the comic realism of his characters and plots, and his own willingness to exaggerate and to risk sentimentality or melodrama, especially in his more recent novels.

Indeed, it seems as if Irving's later novels in some sense attempt to repudiate the formal experimentation of the earlier novels—for example, in choosing not "to mess up the . . . linear narrative of a book anymore"—but, as I have suggested, it is not a fully successful attempt. This is where one can, I think, begin to unravel the telling contradictions in Irving's aesthetics and his fiction. Irving repeatedly formulates an apparently irresolvable opposition between Dickensian narrative and metafiction; as the examples here show, his undampened enthusiasm for one and his disparagement of the other are plain in many of his interviews and essays. His texts—and his critics—however, conflate the two quite comfortably. Carol Harter and James Thompson reason that Irving "experiment[s] with the limits of traditional forms in an attempt to discover how malleable and adaptable they are to a thoroughly modern vision of experience"; they believe that he employs art in general and writing in particular as metaphors for human attempts to "deal with the chaos that defines human experience." Jerome Klinkowitz goes so far as to argue that "the central purpose of Irving's art" is "that fiction cannot be *just* about the act or theory of writing, but must incorporate the act or theory into a fiction that's still about life." There is certainly precedent for this; Patricia Waugh, for example, suggests that "much British self-conscious fiction . . . manages to suggest the fictionality of 'reality' without entirely abandoning realism." But I think that the apparent contradiction between aesthetics and practice may be too easily smoothed out; examined in its contrary form, it proves a fruitful background against which to see some of the obsessions in Irving's fiction.

Harold Bloom's provocative theory of literary genealogy, *The Anxiety of Influence*, can begin to make sense of this contradiction. Bloom's central thesis is that "Poetic history . . . [is] indistinguishable from poetic influence, since strong poets make that history by misreading one another, so as to clear imaginative space for themselves." Bloom's idea of "misreading" is his way of translating into the terms of literary history the relations between precursors and those who follow them, which he sees to be modelled on the oedipal relationship. To misread implies that one is both compelled toward the precursor's texts and compelled to change them—to misinterpret, distort, or revise—so as to forge one's own artistic identity. It is this ambivalence, revisionism, and attendant anxiety that I see operating in Irving's case toward the authority of his forefathers in both the nineteenth century and the mid-twentieth, causing him to reinvent them and their work, creating in his texts the romance of his origins. As a young writer in the 1960s and at school at the Iowa Writers' Workshop, he was naturally enough affected by the formal experimentation of writers just then gaining critical attention and has even used the paternal metaphor to describe his relationship to his mentors. But Irving discounts metafiction as possessing

> no narrative, no characters, no *information*—novels that are just an
> intellectually discursive text with lots of style. . . . Their subject *is*

their technique. And their vision? They have no vision, no private version of the world; there is only a private version of style, of technique.

Here, Irving attempts to reject his "sonship," in Bloom's terms, to the arbiters of late twentieth-century aesthetic values in order to return to the older representatives of traditional Victorian realism. It is a search to supplant the stepfather, as it were, with the absent father, subject to idealization because at greater remove, as an authority in the production of fictive discourse. The search results in part because of Irving's desire for "vision," expressed above, but more particularly it might be seen as a nostalgic flight toward the greater certainties of Victorian representation, which in Irving's reading seems to presuppose a moral system as the structuring context for narrative. In a sense, one might see the manifestations of metafiction in Irving's work as irruptions from the unconscious of the contemporary epistemology—which defines "reality" as linguistic construction rather than as transcendental truth—into the more sure epistemologies of Dickensian realism, where actions exist outside language and have predictable moral consequences.

But like all quests for the missing father, Irving's is fraught with perils. As Bloom suggests, it is impossible simply to accept the authority of the precursor, to become the father. Moreover, to search for Dickens, as the paterfamilias of Victorian fiction, is also to come up short against the absence of Dickens as a representational force in contemporary belief and narrative strategies. Irving cannot write Dickens's novels, and certainly cannot write them in the late twentieth century without altering their meanings (an exercise worthy of Borges's Pierre Menard), nor could he wish to. To oversimplify, then, Irving misreads Dickens by incorporating metafictional techniques, which imply non-Victorian epistemologies, and he misreads the metafictionists by rewriting their linguistic centering of narrative.

None of this would be especially compelling were it not for two things: Irving's preoccupation in his novels with fathers—absent fathers, unknown fathers, surrogate fathers, dangerous fathers—and the vehemence and frequency with which he speaks and writes about his tastes. The latter suggests his investment in positioning himself among his forefathers, what Bloom might term his anxiety (although his protestations surely also reflect the kinds of questions he receives from interviewers). Irving's forceful and repeated enunciation of his aesthetic may in part be his answer to critics who belittle his work for its popularity and accessibility; more important, however, is its indication not of neurosis but of a desire, like that of any artist, to situate his own originality among competing beliefs and aesthetics.

But it may also signal some work of repression. In this respect, it is worth noting in passing a detail in Irving's biography which may offer a clue to some of these contradictions. Irving was raised by his mother and stepfather, a teacher of Russian history at Phillips Exeter Academy in New Hampshire and the man whom he thinks of as his father. His biological father was a flyer in the Second World War who survived the war after being shot down over Burma, but whose whereabouts and name are unknown to Irving. Irving's fascination with paternal origins would be no surprise, then, given the powerful influence on the imagination of such facts. Yet when Gabriel Miller asked him in 1981 whether he might "psychoanalyze" himself on the basis of the recurrent "dead, absent, or indifferent" fathers in his fiction, Irving eluded a personal response in favor of a sociological answer. That very evasion seems to confirm the imaginative significance of fathers in Irving's invention of his fictional world.

While one might say, then, that Irving's preoccupation with fathers, artistic or otherwise, is overdetermined, in Freud's sense, by biography and literary and intellectual history, I do not presume to diagnose the writer. Rather, I hope to discover the sources of distinctive features in Irving's work and uncover their importance. Dianne Sadoff's psychoanalytic study of fatherhood in Dickens, Eliot, and Brontë provides a useful analogy:

> I understand Freud's "primal fantasies" as a metaphor in literary criticism which facilitates interpretation of certain recurring problems in a novelist's work. I do not intend to imply that writing is regressive, because I believe it is not; nor do I mean to imply in appropriating psychoanalysis as a tool for literary interpretation that the writer is "neurotic."

However significant the father has been in Irving's life, the real interest in this figure lies in his symbolic power as origin of and authority over narrative and artistic identity. In this respect, Irving follows his "father," Dickens, in illustrating "the son's attempt to symbolize the father and so position himself as subject in a social, cultural, and linguistic system," with the ultimate aim to "beget or engender himself without the help of fathers, to make himself subject to himself and subject in narrative." Paternal authority is thus conceived in metaphoric relation to the power to narrate. Such a metaphor derives from thinking like Edward Said's when, in this meditation on the beginning conditions of narrative, he conflates "authority," "author," and "auctor" ("increaser") etymologically; he defines the author as "a person who originates or gives existence to something, a begetter, beginner, father, or ancestor." Here, of course, the language emphasizes patrilineal authority.

Despite Irving's sensitivity to female experience, and despite the fact that he often gives prominent place to mothers, especially in relation to their sons (*Garp* and *Owen Meany* provide two obvious examples), the central mystery, obvious gap, or motivation of many of the novels concerns fathers or fatherly figures. That is, one of Irving's major preoccupations emerges from a question about origins—both familial origins and narrative origins.

Perhaps the most obvious recurrence in Irving's novels is, as I have mentioned, of absent or unknown fathers. The conflicts that result may be explicitly developed in the drama of the text, or they may simply act as implicit pressures on the character who is in the position of orphaned or ignorant son, but in each case they speak to the son's attempts to establish himself as the subject of his own story. As early as *Setting Free the Bears*, Irving devoted a significant portion of the narrative to Siggy's musings about where and whom he came from. The central section, Siggy's "Notebook," revolves around his attempt to reconstruct his "pre-history," that is, the story of his parents' meeting, marrying, and conceiving him, in the context of eastern European historical events. Siggy frames the story of his origins by appealing to the influence of two "fathers." His symbolic father is the heroic Zahn Glanz, his mother's first—and only passionate—lover, who disappears in the Anschluss; about him, Siggy writes: "I wouldn't want to say . . . that I've condemned my mother for not letting Zahn Glanz father me. Because even if it wasn't carried in the genes, something of Zahn Glanz certainly got into me. I only want to show how Zahn Glanz put an idea of me in my mother." While "Glanz" means brightness in German, the phallic pun—glans—could hardly have escaped Irving in naming this figure of potency. Siggy yearns for this origin, for the elusive sign of masculine power in the world to give a benediction to his actions and to the identity he has constructed for himself as a renegade. His representation of his biological father shows a falling off from the dream of Zahn Glanz: Vratno Javotnik is a circumspect intellectual, a linguist who accomplishes his "sly survival" in the war rather than making heroic gestures. Zahn Glanz, then, is the fantasized absent "father" for Siggy, the focus of his family romance. Siggy's conflicted sense of origin and resistance to the passivity of his "real" father cause him to try to reinvent his life's narrative in action and in constructing his texts. He plans the novel's final escapade, the freeing of the animals from the Vienna zoo (which plan, after Siggy's death, must be carried out by Graff, the narrator of the sections of the novel that bracket Siggy's texts; Siggy, in turn, becomes Graff's own fantasized father). His plan not only symbolically avenges the murder of Vratno, but in a sense duplicates that murder (in oedipal terms) by transferring his homage to the spirit of Zahn Glanz. Zahn Glanz can therefore be seen as the origin of Irving's narrative, authorizing the exploits Graff narrates as well as the autobiography Siggy writes. Irving represents ambivalence toward the "real" father, far from ideal, who is displaced by the heroic source of narrative. In this sense, it is as much the father's absence—his retreat into legend—as his presence that gives him his authority.

While the absent father is at least a storied figure in *Setting Free the Bears*, he is literally unknown in three other novels by Irving. Garp knows his father's name, but it is all he knows about the ball turret gunner whose semen impregnates Jenny Fields, and even the name is incomplete; Garp's first initials, T. S., are simply an abbreviation for the gunner's rank as Technical Sergeant. Yet perversely enough, it is Technical Sergeant Garp who originates both the life Garp leads and the fiction he writes, each of which is structured by the violence of Garp's conception and his father's death. Unlike the archetypal plot of discovery defined by the story of Oedipus, however, *The World According to Garp* includes no quest to know the father by narrative's end. The father becomes a curious gap in the text, supplanted by the maternal authority of Jenny Fields and by the eventual "feminization" of Garp. Garp approximates female subjectivity when he is figuratively raped (in injury to his family after marital infidelity, injury which he sees as analogous to rape) and when he adopts a female persona to appear at his mother's funeral in drag. In *The World According to Garp*, Irving seems to imply that paternal authority is at worst destructive, at best insignificant. Only in reading the subtext of narrative formation—the novel's evolution from the rape and death of the ball turret gunner—can we uncover the power of paternal origins to create the son's subjectivity, but that power is only reproduced symbolically, never literally, in the text.

One might say, then, that insofar as there is any overt potential for oedipal conflict in the novel, it is over before it starts, but this strange lack of curiosity about origin in *Garp* looks even more like repression of the knowledge of the father's power once one turns to *A Prayer for Owen Meany*. One of the signal facts of that novel is the mystery of John Wheelwright's natural father. Tabby Wheelwright conceives her son but blithely tells no one the source of the child—not her mother, not her husband, married later, and not her son himself—before she dies unexpectedly. John Wheelwright's ambivalence about discovering his father's identity is sign—and, perhaps, cause—of his characteristic passivity; curious when young, he seems to lose interest, and has to be prodded by Owen Meany, a voice from beyond the grave, to recognize his father at last. But this ambivalence is key in the overall design of the narrative. Although the "discovery" is placed conventionally, toward the end of the novel, it is mostly stripped of its drama, its authority over the events of the narrative, and its power to illuminate identity, in part because, unlike Siggy, John has not romanticized his origins. His disappointment in finding that the ineffectual Reverend Lewis Merrill is his father and his rejection of filial connection to Merrill, while apparently fulfilling the oedipal plot by symbolically slaying the father, in fact fail to accomplish the oedipal aim, which is to individuate himself, apart from paternal identity. John ironically fails to recognize his resemblance to his father's passive and detached personality, repressing this opportunity for insight. The only reason he admits for narrating his discovery is that to him the episode represents a "miracle": he believes that he hears Rev. Merrill speaking in Owen Meany's voice in order to expose himself as John's father. John's family romance is thereby displaced from paternal authority into what he interprets as representing divine authority—from the father to the Father. The secular knowledge gained, in itself, is no endpoint at all. In a larger sense, then, *A Prayer for Owen Meany* resists what Sadoff calls the "double narrative temporality" of Dickensian fiction, which drives toward a discovery at the end of the novel even while tracking back toward the novel's origin by "establishing the retrospective evidence of origin throughout the narrative." That is, Irving shows little drive toward exposing origin as one of the aims of his narrative. In this manner, he "misreads" the Dickensian plot of absent paternity by disrupting its control over the narrative.

To different effect, the same thing happens in *The Cider House Rules*, the other of Irving's novels to feature the conspicuous absence of a father. Here, the plight of orphans who lack the social identity conferred by parents is represented by Homer Wells. Here, too, the desire for knowledge in the narrative is displaced toward the maternal alone; in an orphanage where women come and go, unaccompanied by men, it is the mother as source about whom Homer muses. While Homer's own father is suppressed—a gap that will never be filled, and with no regret on Homer's part—fatherhood is nevertheless represented problematically in the novel. Senior Worthington, paterfamilias (as his name suggests) of the Edenic apple orchard, is rendered impotent, his memory enfeebled by Alzheimer's disease until he becomes literally absent in death. Mr. Rose evokes another configuration in the oedipal drama when he rapes and impregnates his own daughter. Even Ray Kendall, idealized as loving father and mechanical wizard, sinks into impotent silence in the face of his daughter's deceptions with Homer, and such masculine-identified power as he has—in his genius with machines—is undermined when he blows himself up with a torpedo. Among natural fathers, nothing seems to exist between impotence and rapaciousness, except for Homer Wells himself, whose loving relationship with his son, Angel, is significantly disrupted by his erasure of himself as father. For fifteen years, he lives a lie by denying that he is Angel's father, and one of the goals of the narrative is to expose this lie to Homer himself, to make him accept his own fatherhood. But even in that exposure is ambivalence. Irving suppresses the revelatory scene we've been waiting for. All Homer says to Angel is that "It's time you knew the whole story," and the scene shifts; the son is given no chance to respond, to uncover the complexity and damage of the father's evasions. The effect is deflation and anticlimax, a rather awkward refusal to satisfy our curiosity. Immediately after Homer's unnarrated confession, he departs the scene to take up his mentor's former position at the orphanage. That is, he never lives in a normalized, acknowledged paternal relation to his son. Irving suggests one of two things: either the impossibility of fathers living in just relation to sons, or the impossibility of himself imagining such fathers. If the latter, one may argue that the failure to imagine paternal authority is responsible for weakening the novel's thrust toward moral disclosure so that one thread of the narrative—that involving the discovery to Angel of his father's identity—collapses in on itself.

In this regard, it is interesting to note the paradox that this is the novel that most fully attempts to imagine Irving's own paternal origin: Wally Worthington is, like Irving's nameless progenitor, a World War II flyer who is shot down over Burma. His story becomes a significant set-piece in the narrative. Irving's own family romance conceives Wally as a blonde Adonis of the orchards, handsome, athletic, and innocent. The idealized projection of the absent father, however, is undercut when Wally comes home from the war, his moral innocence intact, but his physical power virtually destroyed: he is paralyzed and has been rendered sterile. In these particular injuries, then, this symbolized father depicts absence as well as, perhaps, oedipal revenge for it (a "castration" of sorts); at the same time, the novel expresses ambivalence by forgiving that absence, locating its cause outside the otherwise ideal father's will, in powerlessness.

Perhaps because it resists imagining the progenitor as paternal authority, *The Cider House Rules* conjures fathers in other ways. Overtly about the situation of the orphan (one of the Victorians' favorite tropes) and the social plight of mothers who cannot keep their children, the novel's consistently *felt* impulse is to explore fatherly relations, figured in terms of surrogacy. Here, in the displaced paternal relationship, one can uncover more classic oedipal conflict than Irving displays elsewhere. Wilbur Larch, the crusty, dedicated obstetrician, abortionist, and pediatrician residing at St. Cloud's orphanage, conceives an intense fatherly love for Homer Wells. Unable to express this love, except in his increasingly obsessive musings in his journals, he provides a pattern for Homer's own inability to acknowledge his paternity. Nevertheless, unlike Homer, Larch desires—and assumes—paternal authority over his "son," whom he expects to replace him at the orphanage, and he devises an elaborate ruse in order to enable Homer to practice medicine without a license. His plan involves constructing a story for Homer, a narrative to create and explain a new identity. In this Irving enacts the son's fantasy of anxiety over the father's attempts to inscribe his identity and thus to erase his own subjectivity. For his part, Homer at first fulfills the oedipal pattern of resistance by choosing flight from the (surrogate) father; after Larch's death, however, the Victorian morality that structures many of the novel's choices—that is, commitment to duty—supersedes the oedipal conflict in determining narrative closure. Homer capitulates to Larch's plans, assuming the identity of Dr. F. Stone so as to deliver babies and abort fetuses at St. Cloud's. The figure of the Victorian father has the last say. In this later novel, Irving seems more comfortable in determining the fixity of social identity that derives from paternal authority than in opening up the possibility of more fluid subjectivity. This is, of course, in keeping with his debt to his Victorian forefathers.

Surrogacy provides the means of exploring problems of authority in other novels by Irving, generally in the form of a character who seeks direction from another character. In two of Irving's earlier novels, the narrative develops toward rejecting the influence of the romanticized father as false. Because Graff, whose narration in *Setting Free the Bears* encloses Siggy's narratives, lacks Siggy's vitality and imagination (and his narratives are likewise less compelling), he quickly throws in his lot with Siggy, becoming a willing subject to his plans. But insofar as the novel moves toward an illumination, it is that Siggy's conception of freedom—as he hopes to demonstrate it by freeing the animals in the Hietzinger zoo—is blind to the moral and historical complexity that he otherwise begins to identify when he recounts his "pre-history." Just as Graff must finally deny Siggy's authority over his choices, so too does Bogus Trumper in *The Water-Method Man* learn to reject the hold over him of his friend Merrill Overturf. Irving makes it clear that Trumper sees Overturf as his symbolic father when Trumper has a dream in which images of Merrill checking the sugar in his urine are spliced together with images of his own father eating his breakfast. Overturf, who seems to enjoy teetering on the edge of diabetic collapse, is like Siggy in irresponsibly courting death and disaster in his exercises toward autonomy and pleasure. After Trumper's quest for the missing Overturf ends with the information that Merrill has been dead for two years, however, Trumper is essentially freed to return to the fold of familial responsibility. He no longer pursues the illusion that Overturf held out to him, and, like Siggy, Merrill is exposed as making empty gestures toward freedom.

It is therefore not surprising that Irving reuses the name Merrill for the illusory authority of John Wheelwright's father in *A Prayer for Owen Meany*. Nevertheless, when the friend-as-surrogate-father configuration appears in

Owen's relationship to John, one can discern a shift in respect to paternal authority that may be ascribed to Irving's shifting allegiances to his fictional forebears. John Wheelwright clearly depends upon what he interprets as Owen's superior wisdom. Their friendship rarely seems a relation between equals, and as they grow from boys to young men, it increasingly resembles a father-son relationship. John's eagerness to submit to Owen's authority is epitomized when he allows Owen to sever part of his forefinger in order to avoid the draft during the Vietnam war. At the time, John seems to put little thought into the decision, deferring to Owen's reading of his fate. Of course, this act can be seen as a symbolic castration—a figure of which Irving is rather too fond—and, as such, confirms the power of the "father" in the terms of fantasy; John has relinquished himself to the "father" in Owen, just as he relinquishes his own story to narrate Owen's. When Owen dies, John is permanently cast adrift, stripped of identity and sexuality (he becomes something of a eunuch, dedicated to the spiritual power he believes to have been invested in Owen), and willfully exiling himself from the home and people he knows. In a symbolic movement that reverses Homer Wells's trajectory, John demonstrates at the novel's close the significant absence of a paternally bestowed sense of identity and place in society. One can infer in John's fate the obverse of Homer Wells's: the narrative drive is finally toward affirming the father's legitimate claims over the son's identity. Just as it seems likely that Irving's latterday rejection of the technical "showing off" of the early novels implies a rethinking of the gestures toward narrative freedom represented by the metafictionists, so too does the move from denial of paternal authority in the early novels to acceptance of it in *Cider House* and *Owen Meany* seem a direct result of his return to his Victorian forebears in the shaping of fiction.

Still, until the last two novels, the illusory nature of the father's authority is a perspective Irving repeatedly develops on the larger question of father-son relationships. Garp's projected novel. *My Father's Illusions*, about the failures of "an idealistic father who has many children . . . [and] keeps establishing little Utopias for his kids to grow up in," not only expresses his anxiety over protecting his family but also serves as a template for Irving's subsequent novel, *The Hotel New Hampshire*. In that novel, the narrator, John Berry, repeatedly alludes to "my father's illusions" as the structuring influence on his family. Win Berry's illusion is that he can create a haven for his family and a lucrative enterprise by running a resort hotel, a dream planted by his Gatsby-like, visionary sighting of "the man in the white dinner jacket," the owner of a Maine hotel Win is working at as a teenager and the object of Win's own family romance. The result is that Win drags his family from one ruinous site to another—to New Hampshire, where a daughter is raped and Win's father dies, to Vienna, where he loses his wife and a child in transit and the hotel is destroyed by political fanatics, to New York, where another daughter commits suicide, and back to Maine, where he comes to rest, his "blindness" about life made literal. There, the illusion is fulfilled when John accepts his role as caretaker to his father's identity by simply pretending to run the establishment as a hotel. Hotels, the womblike symbol of security and mark of delusion, are unmasked to corroborate John's youthful intuition: "A hotel was a vast ruined space, smelling of fish, guarded by a gun." The fallacy of the father's authority is played out not only in Win Berry's winsome failures—his children learn early that they have to act the parent toward him—but also in the symbolic exposure of Arbuthnot, the original man in the white dinner jacket, to whom Win had relinquished the authority over his own life. Once seen in the flesh rather than as a phantom, Arbuthnot turns out to be a miserly, anti-Semitic embodiment of corruption, his bodily decay representative of his moral degeneracy. The narrative thrust, then, replicates oedipal ambivalence. While John, in his pretense at the last Hotel New Hampshire, allows his father to make him subject to his own (Win's) story, the novel also in both Arbuthnot and Win himself unseats the power of the father as rightful inventor of the family's story—that story which, as I mentioned above, Irving self-consciously shows Win telling in the opening pages of the novel.

The most obvious case among Irving's novels of the son's desire to resist the father's invention of his story appears in *The Water-Method Man*, in Bogus's oedipal relationship to his father, Dr. Edward Trumper. Dr. Trumper's conventional aspiration is for Bogus to earn a stable income in a respected profession—that is, to imitate him—and he cuts Bogus off for failing to meet his standard. Theirs is the stereotypical Victorian relationship, the father distant and disapproving, and Bogus's futile gestures of rebellion, such as mailing a dead duck to him, are apparently unfelt by his father. As in the missing narration of Homer Wells's confession to his son, Irving neither provides Dr. Trumper's responses nor develops the explicit conflict, which might at first suggest that he is suppressing the meaning of their relationship. Instead, however, the conflict is displaced, not least into Bogus's adulation of Merrill Overturf. Most of the conflict is played out symbolically: Trumper dedicates himself to denying origins of various kinds. When he first meets his wife-to-be at an Austrian ski resort, he speaks only German in an effort to disguise his American citizenship. Likewise, his dissertation work on an "Old Low Norse" poem becomes largely an invention. Not only does he invent rather than translate portions of the poem, but he also devises an "etymological dictionary of Old Low Norse," about which he claims, "*I made up a lot of origins*. This made the translation of *Akthelt and Gunnel* easier too.

I started making up a lot of words" (emphasis added). Trumper's misdirected efforts to make up origins, to fashion his own story out of new words, end in failure, and it is only when he recognizes his biological power to create—to father a child as token of commitment to a new relationship—that his narrow, winding road of a life can straighten out. In Irving's plan for resolution, Trumper must become an originator—to reenact his father's procreative gesture—in order to gain authority, rather than try to revise his own origins. The novel's closure combines fatalism (Trumper's anatomy is his destiny) with a dim view of the possibility of devising one's own subjectivity. In its conclusions, *The Water-Method Man* presages Irving's later shift away from modes of metafiction, since Trumper's self-conscious attempts to manipulate his world through language fail, leaving him to confront and affirm a materialist view of authorship.

The question of paternal authority gains its most comprehensively symbolic representation in *A Prayer for Owen Meany*. Here, too, displacement is functioning, but in surprising ways. As I have argued, the fathers in the novel are all absent, or virtually so, but the source of authority becomes absolute because *A Prayer for Owen Meany* places it in the ultimate Father, God. John Wheelwright, the fatherless narrator, opens his narration by implying that the following story will be a conversion narrative: he is "doomed to remember a boy with a wrecked voice . . . because he is the reason I believe in God." In a sense, this novel conflates in a single quest all of the contradictory perspectives on paternity I have discovered in Irving's work, by figuring the father in terms of transcendent authority, the Law. John Wheelwright becomes the disciple and mouthpiece for Owen Meany, who interprets his precognitive experiences to mean that he has been in some sense "chosen": he tells John that "GOD HAS TAKEN YOUR MOTHER. MY HANDS WERE THE INSTRUMENT. GOD HAS TAKEN MY HANDS. I AM GOD'S INSTRUMENT." Owen accepts his perceived role fatalistically; he exhibits doubt only when circumstances suggest to him that his final, heroic act of instrumentality, as he has foreseen it—saving a roomful of children from a grenade—will not take place. Calling it faith, he has in effect accepted the Father's delineation of his identity, at least as he construes it. Both figuratively and, later, literally, he gives up his hands to his God willingly. As a character, Owen's distance from credibility may be measured by his lack of resistance to his intuited fate. John, however, enacts the oedipal drama in relation to the story he vicariously lives through Owen. God is for him the Father who must be either absent, a *deus absconditis*, or malevolent, since He has created the violent world (at which John rails through much of the novel's latter half), leaving humans to their innate capacity for corruption and self-destruction. It is only finally by dint of

Owen's self-sacrifice—the confirmation, at least to John, of the miraculousness of Owen's foresight—that John "finds" the Father. But it is an ambiguous discovery, since John is left drifting in the human world, emotionally sterile and sexually neutered. His recovery of origin does not grant him the power in the worlds of matter or spirit that we have come to expect from the conventions of such a narrative quest.

It is this ambivalence toward the father's power that returns time and again in Irving's novels. In each case, Irving's efforts to imagine paternal origins—of either heroic or ironic dimensions—result in a text that points self-consciously to its own gaps, suppressions, and contradictions. As the central cipher and origin of all narrative in Irving's work, the father wields the power of the oedipal drama both to devise and delimit subjectivity. Irving's inclusion of the complementary phenomena of absent and invented fathers, whose influences both threaten and tempt adoption, maps out the anxiety in relation to paternal authority that also becomes visible in the larger context of Irving's self-placement within literary history. The orphan's romance of origin—the invented father whose control over the narrative of one's life is always absolute, benevolent, known, uncontested—is equivalent to the romance of the self-inventing artist who yet needs to feel that, like Prometheus, he has stolen the tools of his own self-invention.

PHILIP PAGE

Hero Worship and Hermeneutic Dialectics: *John Irving's* A Prayer for Owen Meany

In the Western tradition of hermeneutics, two ways of knowing have often been contrasted. One, usually considered inferior, is a process—earthbound and empirical—which moves logically from step to step, and is communicable, repeatable and transferable. The conclusions reached by this method always remain hypotheses and thus are subject to dispute and revision. The second—presumed superior—form of knowing is an upward leap that relies on unpredictable flashes of insight. Such knowing requires not merely reason and logic but all of our human—often some superhuman—faculties, and as a result tends to be noncommunicable and nonreplicable.

In *The Republic*, for example, Plato distinguishes thinking (dianoia) from intelligence (noesis): with the former the mind "is compelled to pursue its inquiry by starting from assumptions and travelling, not up to a principle, but down to a conclusion," whereas with the latter "the mind moves in the other direction, from an assumption up towards a principle which is not hypothetical." Plato's distinctions are analogous to Milton's "Discursive" and "Intuitive" reason, the former most often used by humans and the latter most often by angels.

Similarly, William James distinguishes between "naturalism" and "supernaturalism," between nonreligious and religious experience. In analyzing Martin Luther's faith, James differentiates between the "intellec-

From *Mosaic* 28 (September 1995). © 1995 by *Mosaic*.

tual" part and the "far more vital" part, "something not intellectual but immediate and intuitive." He associates this second mode with the "affective experience," the "saintly character," and the "mystical state." For James, the religious way of knowing is characterized by its transforming effect, by its inclusion of a broader range of experience than is encompassed by the nonreligious or "rationalistic consciousness," and by its lack of transferability to another human: "Feeling is private and dumb."

More recently, Paul Ricoeur explores the difference between explanation (explication, *Erklarung*) and understanding (comprehension, *Verstandnis*). Borrowed from the natural sciences, the former is "methodic" and proceeds in piecemeal fashion: "in explanation we ex-plicate or unfold the range of propositions and meanings"; explanation consists of "external facts to observe, hypotheses to be submitted to empirical verification, general laws for covering such facts, theories to encompass the scattered laws in a systematic whole, and subordination of empirical generalizations to hypothetic-deductive procedures." In contrast, understanding is "the nonmethodic moment" in which one holistically discovers meaning: "in understanding we comprehend or grasp as a whole the chain of partial meaning in one act of synthesis"; rather than focusing on external facts, it requires "the transference of ourselves into another's psychic life."

For Ricoeur, the two forms of knowing are neither hierarchical nor mutually exclusive, but form a "highly mediated dialectic." The inquiry into a given text proceeds through a "hermeneutical arc": from a preliminary, naive understanding (a "guess"), through an analytic explanation, to a more sophisticated comprehensive understanding. Ricoeur defines this experience of "follow[ing] the path of thought opened by the text" as interpretation (interpretation, *Deutung*), which, by completing the hermeneutical circle, "culminates in the self-interpretation of a subject who thenceforth understands himself better, understands himself differently, or simply begins to understand himself."

In *A Prayer for Owen Meany* (1989), John Irving plays with this hermeneutical dialectic. He sets up an apparent dichotomy between the two traditional ways of knowing, but simultaneously he parodies each approach, unravels the distinction between them, and half-mockingly offers common sense as a third alternative.

Readers are probably most familiar with Irving's earlier novel, *The World According to Garp* (1976), which recounts the comic/tragic life of T. S. Garp, as he attempts to write fiction, protect his family, and come to grips with his own sexuality in the midst of the women's liberation movement. Irving's next two novels, *The Hotel New Hampshire* (1982) and *The Cider-House Rules* (1985), recall *Garp* in their depictions of the profound humor and simultaneous pathos of human life, and in *Rules* Irving broadens his vision by addressing the issues of abortion and adoption.

A Prayer for Owen Meany is the Bildungsroman of John Wheelwright, an expatriate bachelor and English teacher living in Toronto, who retrospectively narrates the effects on his life of his boyhood friend, Owen Meany. The lives of the two boys become entwined when Owen hits a line drive that kills Johnny's mother and when they try to discover the identity of Johnny's real father. During their boyhood in the New England town of Gravesend, the passive and laconic Johnny is fascinated by the remarkable Owen. Owen leads not only Johnny but all the students at their private school, the Gravesend Academy, by his supreme self-confidence and by his commanding and almost unearthly voice (rendered throughout in capital letters). Through a series of visions and dreams, Owen acquires the belief that he has a divine mission which requires him to die on 7 July 1968, in a tropical setting. Owen also takes charge of Johnny's life, helping him through school, directing him toward a career as an English teacher, and amputating his finger to keep him out of the Vietnam War. The plot culminates with Owen's death in a Phoenix airport when he sacrifices himself to save a group of Vietnamese children and nuns. Owen's commanding presence, his apparent prophetic powers and his martyrdom convince John that his friend was literally the "Second Coming."

In *A Prayer for Owen Meany*, the characters, most prominently Johnny and Owen, are confronted with a rich array of signs—objects, events, texts, other characters—which they have difficulty interpreting. From the perspective of semiotics, such difficulty is not surprising. In the early 20th century, for example, Charles S. Peirce argued that there is no simple relationship between a sign and its meaning but instead an infinite regression of signs. Each sign produces in the interpreter something new, what Peirce calls the interpretant, but in turn each interpretant must be named by another sign which has another interpretant, and so on indefinitely. More recently, Jonathan Culler has argued that the traditional distinction between signifier and signified cannot be maintained. Instead of that opposition, there are, always already, both "the differences responsible for meaning" and the systems of concepts and signs "which enable an act to signify." For Culler, semiotics reveals the fundamental contradictions of any mode of inquiry or analysis: "The alternative, then, is not a discussion, not another mode of analysis, but acts of writing, acts of displacement, play which violates language and rationality."

A Prayer for Owen Meany similarly overwhelms readers with a plethora of signs, and calls particular attention to readers' presuppositions about interpreting them. Indirectly, the text foregrounds this issue by the multitude of interpretative acts undertaken by the characters. More directly, Irving's text draws attention to the act of interpretation through its mode of narration. As John retells his life, he unavoidably interprets past events, and this situation forces the reader to consider not only the events but also the way they may be re-constructed through the process of narration. To accentuate this pattern, John habitually addresses the reader, most noticeably in his refrains of "Remember that?" and "as you shall see," which in their shrill insistence force the reader to participate and interpret. Moreover, in its presentation of signs and their interpretations by characters and readers, the novel appears to offer two fundamentally different ways of interpreting, ways which closely resemble Ricoeur's "explanation" and "understanding."

Many characters are said to be avid explainers: Harriet Wheelwright (Johnny's grandmother) tries to interpret everyone in Gravesend and everything on television; Dan Needham (Johnny's step-father) explains why Owen gives his prized set of baseball cards to Johnny; the neighbor Mr. Fish tries to interpret the school's Christmas pageant; and the Wheelwright's maid Germaine sees every event or act as a sign of some deeper spiritual presence. More significantly, much of the plot revolves around the identity of Johnny's biological father, and Johnny and Owen (led by Owen) conduct an elaborate detective-like investigation of the issue, explaining the few relevant clues and following up their thin leads in a step-by-step manner. For example, as methodical and reasonable investigators, they infer that, since Johnny's mother (Tabitha) met his step-father on the train from Boston, she may also have met Johnny's biological father there. Since that clue is nearly impossible to pursue, they also infer that she may have met the biological father during her mysterious weekly trips to Boston, which sends them on a wild goose chase to the bar where Tabitha used to sing.

The things to be explained vary widely. They include characters: for example, Dan, the Reverend Merrill, Johnny himself, and nearly everyone the grown-up John knows in Toronto. Owen, as the central mystery, is the most frequently analyzed character. His unearthly voice requires explanation, and his opinions as "The Voice" are always examined. John as well as other characters use a variety of metaphors to figure Owen. Many metaphors for Owen are other-worldly (Chosen One, angel, god, devil, Jesus Christ, Antichrist), and he plays the parts of Jesus and the Ghost of Christmas Future. Other metaphors place him in a special category of people (holy man, martyr, prophet, child-pharaoh) or associate him with emblematic figures (a figurehead on a ship, a scarecrow, a gnome). Still others compare him to a small animal—bird, water bug, possum, fish, fox, butterfly, mouse. He is also something to be lifted or hugged (a doll).

This extensive range of metaphors for Owen establishes him as the primary sign to be explained, by the other characters and by the reader. The array of metaphors, however, suggests the impossibility of any consistent explanation of Owen and, by extension, of the novel: if he can be

Christ or Antichrist, fox or water bug, holy man or gnome, what is he? And if his essence is unclear, he must be forever analyzed, must be forever part of Peirce's infinite regression of signs and interpretants.

Even more noticeably than characters, objects and events are repeatedly subjected to explanation. One such object is the drawing of an apparently armless man which had served as the signature of the local 17th-century Indian chief, Watahantowet, on the documents ceding the Gravesend area to the original white settlers. This totem of the armless man is the ur-instance of the armless, fingerless, clawless motif that pervades the novel. Just as Watahantowet's totem is a mysterious and highly disputed sign, so Owen's totem—his baseball card collection—is open for inquiry, especially when it appears to reveal his feelings about the death of Johnny's mother. His collection, his most prized possession, inspires interpretative awe in the other kids: "the cards were alphabetized, or ordered under another system—all the infielders together, maybe. We didn't know what the system was, but obviously Owen had a system." Owen's giving of his collection to Johnny must then be explained, along with Johnny's answering gift of his most prized possession, a stuffed armadillo, and then the cycle continues when Owen returns the armadillo—without its claws—to Johnny. Similar fates await other rich signs, such as Tabitha's dressmaker's dummy which Owen mistakes for the ghost of Tabitha herself, the Volkswagen of the absurd psychologist, Dr. Dolder, which Owen arranges to be placed on the school's auditorium stage, the statue of Mary Magdalene whose arms Owen removes, and the fatal baseball which becomes the central clue in the hunt for Johnny's real father.

Owen is not only the prime character to be explained (in Peirce's terms, the prime interpretant) but also the prime investigator. For example, when, detective-like, he and Johnny inspect the empty dormitory rooms at Gravesend Academy, Owen creates each boy's personality from the clues left in the room. His method is thorough and orderly: he examines every item, always completes his investigation by lying on the absent boy's bed, and then draws his conclusions.

In addition to characters and objects, various texts in the novel are subjected to investigation. As the grown-up narrator, John bases much of his explanation of Owen on the latter's diary, an embedded text in which Owen had attempted to explain the events in his life. Many of Owen's and John's conclusions about Owen's mission in life focus on another text—the inscription of the date of his death which he claims to see on the tombstone in the community production of *A Christmas Carol*. Owen is always the primary explainer, not only of the tombstone but of other texts such as Christmas carols and an Army field manual.

The novel also alludes to and often includes comments on other literary texts, chiefly *The Great Gatsby* and the novels of Thomas Hardy. The references to Fitzgerald's novel suggest parallels between Nick Carraway—the bystander who narrates the story of his idol, Jay Gatsby—and John's relationship to his idol, Owen Meany. The several allusions to Hardy imply that his determinism is comparable to both Owen's emerging conviction that his life is fated and John's necessity to believe in the miraculousness of Owen's life and its effect on his own life. In turn, references to contemporary literature, movies, television and popular music relate the question of interpretation to American culture, and within this context to the effect of the Vietnam war on America and, as Sean French asserts, about America's loss of innocence after that war. John reaches maturity during that crisis, and his inability to come to grips with it and therefore with America contribute greatly to his bitterness.

If the question of Johnny's paternity is the first major issue to be investigated, the question of Owen's possible divinity is the second. Does he indeed have foreknowledge of his death, does he perform a miracle in saving the Vietnamese children, does he "speak" to John after his death, does he ascend to Heaven when he dies, was his conception indeed immaculate as his own father claims?

Such issues cannot be investigated through the methodical process of explanation, but require the other traditional way of discovering meaning—in Ricoeur's terminology, understanding, and in the novel's terms, faith. When one understands, it is intuitive and holistic. Either one has faith—that is, one believes without question—or one does not. The experience is unutterable and unsharable: as Owen says, "THE REAL MIRACLES AREN'T ANYTHING YOU CAN SEE—THEY'RE THINGS YOU HAVE TO BELIEVE WITHOUT SEEING." One of John's reasons for believing in Owen's divinity is his sense of the dead Owen's presence in his life, in particular on the occasion when he felt that Owen had kept him from falling down a stairway. Yet when John tries to convince his stepfather of Owen's intervention, Dan does not deny his account of his sensations but replies, "But you can't expect me to believe that Owen Meany's actual hand kept you from falling down those cellar stairs; you can't expect me to be convinced that Owen Meany's actual voice 'spoke' to you in the secret passageway."

Faith or understanding as an alternative to explanation is not limited to John's belief in Owen's divinity. Owen's faith in his divine mission and predestined death is a total, instantaneous leap based on inward vision and signs that are not apparent to anyone else and hence are not communicable or reproducible. The "evidence" that these signs provide must be accepted on faith or intuition, not through a process of explanation or investigation. The data is not external "facts" but internal mental experience. Similarly, the novel raises the question of one's faith in one's country. Both Johnny and Owen, especially Owen, and by extension their generation, initially believe in the United States, its government and President Kennedy. Their belief is holistic, not a result of a process of explanation, and their faith then is tested by the revelations of Kennedy's affair with Marilyn Monroe. Both lose their naive faith, but Owen rechannels his into a personal and divinely inspired mission, whereas John, never recovering from the loss, becomes neurotically embittered toward his country, his life and people in general.

Although at first glance Irving seems to suggest that explanation and faith/understanding are distinct ways of knowing, a closer look reveals that he does not neatly distinguish the two modes, but like Ricoeur sees them as a "highly mediated dialectic." For example, although Johnny and Owen seem to follow a discursive and presumably rational exploration of signs in their attempts to solve the riddle of his biological father, an element of faith plays a crucial role in that investigation. When Johnny looks over the audience during a performance of *A Christmas Carol*, he senses a resemblance between this audience and the crowd at the fatal baseball game; and in doing so, he feels that his father must have been the person at the game to whom Tabitha was waving when she was hit by Owen's batted ball and therefore that he will be able to recognize his father in the audience at the play. Even though Johnny does not find his father at this point, his leap to the idea that his father must have been the person to whom Tabitha was waving becomes a significant factor in his and Owen's investigation. What is necessary for his sudden sensation is the internal intuition of faith rather than the external process of explanation, as Owen's response to Johnny's theory confirms: "As for my 'imagining' that my mother had been waving to my actual father in the last seconds she was alive, Owen Meany believed in trusting such instincts; he said that I must be ON THE RIGHT TRACK, because the idea gave him THE SHIVERS—a sure sign." Similarly, during Owen's otherwise empirical investigation of the Academy boys' empty rooms in the school dormitory—in which he is "so systematic in his methods of search, so deliberate about putting everything back exactly where it had been"—nevertheless "His behavior in the rooms was remindful of a holy man's search of a cathedral of antiquity—as if he could divine some ancient and also holy intention there."

As these examples suggest, in Irving's novel the two ways of knowing become indistinguishable: "imagining" blends with investigating, feelings are as essential as thought, external "facts" merge with internal projections, the hermeneutical circle is completed. One "knows" because one believes, because one experiences an uncontrollable, unsharable physiological response, such as the shivers, which is a recurrent indication of this blending of the two modes.

In addition to this blurring of the distinction between the two alleged poles, each term is itself undercut. In the case of the explanatory mode, the flashback that recounts Chief Watahantowet and his ambiguous "signature" best illustrates such parodying:

> The local sagamore's name was Watahantowet; instead of his signature, he made his mark upon the deed in the form of his totem—an armless man. Later, there was some dispute—not very interesting—regarding the Indian deed, and more interesting speculation regarding why Watahantowet's totem was an armless man. Some said it was how it made the sagamore feel to give up all that land—to have his arms cut off—and others pointed out that earlier "marks" made by Watahantowet revealed that the figure, although armless, held a feather in his mouth; this was said to indicate the sagamore's frustration at being unable to write. But in several other versions of the totem ascribed to Watahantowet, the figure has a tomahawk in its mouth and looks completely crazy—or else, he is making a gesture toward peace: no arms, tomahawk in mouth; together, perhaps, they are meant to signify that Watahantowet does not fight.

First, there is a sign, a written mark, a totem. That particular sign is then "open to interpretation and dispute," regarding the nature of the signifier and the signified, as well as the motives behind the sign and its investigation. Yet neither the signifier nor the signified can be pinned down: in endless Peircean fashion more signs proliferate (armless/unarmed, feather/tomahawk) as rapidly as do the explanations of those signs. The supposed original sign and any systematic attempt at explaining it thus unravel. As Wendy Steiner has noted, there are numerous parallels between this novel and Hawthorne's *The Scarlet Letter*, of which the most significant is the proliferation of signs and attempted explanations. Watahantowet's mark functions like the scarlet letter A. Like the Chief's mark, more and more A's (may) appear—in the sky, on Dimmesdale's chest, on the narrator's brain—and their explanations multiply throughout the book and in the voluminous criticism on it. Both Watahantowet's sign and the letter A exemplify Culler's assertion of the breakdown between signifier and signified.

In *A Prayer*, the explanatory mode is undercut in countless additional ways. It is parodied in Germaine, who sees all things as signs of supernatural influence over human lives; for example, "Owen himself was taken as a 'sign' by poor Germaine; his diminutive size suggested to her that Owen was small enough to actually enter the body and soul of another person—and cause that person to perform unnatural acts." Explanation is reduced to the farcical when Owen's girlfriend Hester vomits on New Year's Eve and he sees it as a sign of the bad year to come and when Hester interprets one of the fireworks as looking "like sperm." More seriously, the elaborate process of explaining the clues about Johnny's father is undercut when the investigation culminates in the anti-climax of Johnny's discovery that the Reverend Merrill is his biological father. Instead of feeling relief and joy at finally finding his father, Johnny feels only scorn for Mr. Merrill, largely because the latter's religious beliefs seem superficial to him.

Yet, just as explanation as a way of knowing is both present and undercut, so is faith/understanding. Faith is mocked when John reports that no hailstones strike Owen during the hailstorm at Dan and Tabitha's wedding. Nor can faith be taken seriously when the details of the Holy Nativity become the ingredients for comic debunking, as in the episode in which the rector and his wife Barb wrangle with Owen about the school's Christmas pageant:

> "[THE TURTLEDOVES] LOOK LIKE THEY'RE FROM OUTER SPACE," Owen said. "NO ONE KNOWS WHAT THEY'RE SUPPOSED TO BE."
>
> "They're doves!" Barb Wiggin said. "Everyone knows what doves are!"
>
> "THEY'RE GIANT DOVES," Owen said. "THEY'RE AS BIG AS HALF A DONKEY. WHAT KIND OF BIRD IS THAT? A BIRD FROM MARS? THEY'RE ACTUALLY KIND OF FRIGHTENING."
>
> "Not everyone can be a king or a shepherd or a donkey, Owen," the rector said.

The debunking of faith is perhaps most evident in the treatment of the town's two ministers, Reverend Wiggin and Reverend Merrill. For the former, faith is a constant battle, to be verified not by contentment or inner harmony but by how vigorously one lives and prays: "And he loved all allusions to faith as a battle to be savagely fought and won; faith was a war waged against faith's adversaries." More interesting is Reverend Merrill, whose "faith" is initially based not on belief but on doubt: "he reassured us that doubt was the essence of faith, and not faith's opposite." In the old logic of binary opposites, this makes no sense. Faith cannot be based on doubt unless they are not opposites, unless their apparent difference is undermined; so Irving proceeds to unravel the distinction as he twists and retwists this faith/doubt paradox.

Plagued by his lack of what he considers true faith, a lack manifested by his stutter, Reverend Merrill abandons his so-called faith based on doubt, gains what he thinks is true faith and loses the stutter. His conversion, however, is the direct result of a trick played by Johnny: he makes Merrill believe that the latter has seen the dead Tabitha and that the fatal baseball has miraculously reappeared. Johnny, already disenchanted with Merrill as a father, is further disgusted by what he sees as Merrill's unconvincing conversion, and Irving and the reader are likely to share Johnny's skepticism. Thus, Merrill's faith in God and his doubt, like Watahantowet's mark and its endless interpretations, are not static, not unidimensional, not separable. The result is that understanding as well as explanation, like signifier and signified, are present but not present, are always already being denied even as they are asserted.

In addition to blurring the distinction between explanation and understanding, and besides calling into question both ways of knowing, Irving offers a third alternative which further depolarizes the opposition. When confronted with a perplexing sign or with the need to understand or believe, some characters refuse either approach but instead simply accept the phenomenon as a given, a non-sign, a bare thing without meaning or implication. Owen's girlfriend Hester is the primary exemplar of this common-sense approach. Refusing to find any explanations for what she encounters and being without any faith, she accepts life at face value and argues passionately with Owen for the way that he takes life seriously and symbolically. Before Owen's death, Johnny often adopts a similar position. For example, whereas Owen finds each boy's room in the dormitory a treasure trove of interpretable signs, Johnny is skeptical: "They're just things. . . . What can we tell about the guy who lives here, really?" Even Owen sometimes demonstrates this literalism, for example when he insists on removing the crib from the creche in the nativity scene for the Christmas pageant because of the line, "No crib for his bed," in the carol "Away in a Manger." This third way of knowing recalls Flask in Melville's *Moby-Dick*, who looks at the otherwise richly interpreted doubloon and "see[s] nothing here, nothing but a round thing made of gold." Things are just things, not signs, neither open to explanation nor available as vehicles for understanding.

This skeptical approach resembles Clifford Geertz's analysis of common sense. Common sense, he argues, is a culturally determined set of constructs or assumptions which vary from culture to culture but which people in each culture assume to be beyond question. Common sense "rests its [case] on the assertion that it is not a case at all." Modifying Wittgenstein's comparison of language to a city, Geertz compares culture to a city, in which the core is "the ancient tangle of received practices, accepted beliefs, habitual judgments, and untaught emotions" of a culture—that is, the domain principally of faith or understanding. Geertz contrasts this core with the city's suburbs—"those squared off and straightened out systems of thought and action"—such as "physics, counterpoint, existentialism, Christianity, engineering, jurisprudence, Marxism," in short the domain of explanation.

Geertz argues that common sense has usually been considered unquestionable, as encompassing that which every sane person in every culture would accept: that is, as common truths not requiring explanation. As he sees it, however, common sense is equally a cultural system, "as much an interpretation of the immediacies of experience, a gloss on them, as are myth, painting, epistemology, or whatever . . . [and] can be questioned, disputed, affirmed, developed, formalized, contemplated, even taught. . . ." Therefore he places common sense between the core and the rest of the suburbs, "as one of the oldest suburbs of human culture—not very regular, not very uniform, but moving beyond the maze of little streets and squares toward some less casual shape."

Geertz's analysis suggests that such categories as common sense and culturally specific disciplines are not as distinct as one might presuppose, and in *A Prayer for Owen Meany*, Irving suggests the same with respect to explanation versus faith, discursive versus intuitive reasoning, nonreligious versus religious experience. Instead of adhering to any bipolar opposition, Irving devalues each extreme, documenting the danger of relying too heavily on either term of each opposition. By doing so, he thus aligns himself with mainstream poststructuralist thought and specifically with Ricoeur's insistence on the whole interpretative process, the "highly mediated dialectic" between explanation and understanding.

In Irving's novel, the deconstruction of the two traditional ways of knowing is one manifestation of a broader pattern of the posing and then merging of apparent bipolar oppositions. Another manifestation of this pattern involves gender. In *The World According to Garp*, both strident maleness and strident femaleness fail miserably: the sexual aggression of assorted males, the radical responses to that aggression by many females, and Garp's own gender-related intensity manifest this theme. As Carol C. Harter and James R. Thompson assert, Garp moves toward the integration of the masculine and the feminine in a more mature self. By the end of the novel, sexual extremism has been devalued and deflated, replaced by a valued group of androgynous or sexually benign characters—Roberta Muldoon, Ellen James, Duncan Garp and young Jenny Garp.

In *A Prayer for Owen Meany*, gender roles and gender relations, especially those pertaining to fathers and mothers and wives and husbands, are again paramount. As in Garp, most of the women and men fail as parents or partners: the Meanys, the Wiggins and the Merrills are hopelessly weak parents; the Dowlings parodically try to reverse gender roles; and the Brinker-Smiths engage in a mockery of lovemaking and childrearing. Individually, most men and women fail to develop healthy gender identities: for example, there is Mr. Peabody's effeminacy, Mr. Tubulari's machismo, Mrs. Lish's aggressive femininity and Mary Beth Baird's smothering of Owen.

Gender terms also define John Wheelwright's failure to mature. His failure is connected to his frustrated search for his biological father as well as for historical "founding fathers," for political father figures (Presidents Kennedy and Reagan) and for God the father. Finding none of these, he substitutes Owen, but he pays heavily for this displacement, and the price includes his self-exile to Canada and his incurable immaturity. His failure is also connected to his refusal to engage in sexual intercourse and, more dramatically, to his emasculation when Owen amputates Johnny's finger and the latter passively accepts his symbolic castration. Unable to find a true father, he is cut off from fatherhood, thus completing his alienation from society. He is symbolically genderless, lost in a self-defeating confusion of identity. The sexually benign characters in Garp, as well as Owen, gain spiritual strength from their androgyny, but for John the loss of the male/female gender dichotomy leads to the abdication of adulthood and to impotent stagnation.

As opposed to the armlessness of Chief Watahantowet's mark and to the armlessness of Owen just before he dies, most men in the world around Johnny, far from abdicating their manhood, express it in war: they bear arms against each other. This unchecked masculine drive to compete and conquer culminates in the appropriately named Dick Jarvits, the Vietnam veteran who becomes a loaded, phallic weapon intent on killing everything Vietnamese, even the children and the nuns at the Phoenix airport.

Steiner asserts that at the end of Garp Roberta finds a viable middle position between unchecked gender aggression and emasculation, and the other androgynous characters at the end of Garp, as well as Owen, also find this middle position. Owen personifies Irving's validation of androgyny and benign sexuality: he is powerful yet unthreatening, he is sexually active and yet self-sacrificing, and he is genitally well-endowed yet doll-like. His physical appeal transcends gender—no one can resist touching him. He triumphs by losing his arms and thus symbolically by rejecting the destructive armaments of other men and the country. In complete contrast to John, Owen does reconcile gender dichotomies.

The undermining of apparent dichotomies is apparent not only in the gender theme but also in the novel's narrative format. On the one hand, there is the story itself (the fabula), the story of Johnny and Owen growing up. On the other hand, there is the discourse or narration (the syuzhet), John the narrator retelling his life story from Toronto. At first (and always to some extent) these two modes are distinct. After a three-paragraph introduction of his narrative, John relates the events of the story with, at first, only occasional references to himself as narrator. Then, beginning on page 87, he interjects sections containing information about his present life in Toronto. These discourse sections appear to be distinct from the story sections, separated from them by a blank line and beginning with a diary-like date, such as "Toronto: July 21, 1987." Yet the distinction does not hold up. Even in the first of these sections, and in section after section, John mixes incidents from the so-called story into the so-called discourse. The distinction is never quite lost (readers know the difference between Johnny-the-character and John-the-narrator), yet the textual distinction between story and discourse becomes increasingly indeterminate.

The same pattern of play between two opposed and yet similar poles is suggested by the pseudo-biographical connections between John Wheelwright, the narrator/character, and John Irving, the author. Both "Johns" were born in 1942, both are New Englanders, both attended private academies and both have a Toronto connection; yet most "facts" of their lives differ, and readers are not likely to confuse the historically real status of the author with the fictional status of the character. Yet Irving seems to tease readers with the parallels, to invite speculation about the autobiographical possibilities, to present the opposition and deny it.

Similarly, Irving teases readers with uncertainties about the reliability of John's narration. Like many first-person narrators, he is not always present at the scenes he describes and hence resorts to speculation about what must have happened; without direct access to the other characters' minds he imagines what they must have thought. More unsettling are his occasional confessions of possible inaccuracies in his account, as for example when he wonders: "In addition to not knowing who my father was, what else didn't I know?", or when he admits that he was drunk when he thought that the dead Owen saved him from falling down the stairs, and when he wonders if events are the way he remembers them because "Perhaps Owen had even changed my memory."

In addition to these self-doubts about his narration, on numerous occasions John's interpretations turn out to be wrong: he is sure that Owen will dread meeting his cousins, but Owen is confident and assertive; he thinks that Reverend Merrill's silence around him and Owen is because of the minister's awe of Owen, not because Merrill is John's father; and he initially misinterprets Dick Jarvits as an "overgrown boy" in "workmen's overalls," not the deadly killer he is. The discussion of Nick Carraway in the class that John teaches provides a clue about John's status as narrator. Just as John's student remarks that "I think we're not supposed to trust [Nick]—not completely, I mean," so John's reliability as a narrator, especially as a witness who claims Owen's divinity, is consistently undermined.

Despite this clue and the ironic distancing between John Irving and John Wheelwright, several reviewers seem to conflate them. Patrick Parrinder criticizes John Wheelwright's misanthropic attitudes and sophomoric immaturity as if they reflected the author's position; William Pritchard claims that there is no irony in the narration; and Steiner, asserting that the "narrator is quite obviously Irving's shadow," finds his reminiscences "unspeakably tedious." John Wheelwright is ambiguously similar to John Irving, but he is distinct from the author, not a reflection of him. The grown-up John Wheelwright, having failed to mature beyond his youthful adoration of Owen, is tedious, sententious and obsessive, and/but he has unshakable faith in Owen's divinity. Irving thus problematizes the relationships between author and character/narrator, raises necessary but unresolvable questions about the validity of claims of intuitive understanding and thereby questions faith at the same time as he affirms it.

Irving's strategy of offering ambiguously multiple signs and interpretations is encapsulized with the novel's title itself. On one hand the book is a prayer for Owen, which recalls the poignant scene in which Owen begs Reverend Merrill to offer such a prayer, but on the other hand, it is John who is the "pray-er," and Owen is the object of his supplications. Similarly, Owen Meany's name reverberates with various significations. Do we, the narrator, and/or the other characters "owe" something to Owen? Do we owe him some kind of "meaning"? Or do any of us "own" Owen or his meaning, and/or does Owen himself owe or own any meaning? Furthermore, is Owen a "meany," suggestive not of meaning but of meanness, and is there something mean about withholding meaning? Or is it John who is mean-spirited, narrow and unforgiving? As with the rest of the novel, the questions proliferate and the attempt to formulate answers is undercut: no single interpretation suffices, no simple oppositions remain.

The danger of relying too heavily on either term of traditional oppositions is illustrated most poignantly by John Wheelwright, whose self-exile into bitterness, childishness, self-pity and nostalgia stem from, among other causes, his failure to transcend the logic of binary oppositions. He is stuck in the rigidity of oppositional thinking: for example, that the U.S. must be either perfect or damned, that Owen must be either divine or human, and that his own life must be either wonderful or terrible. John's stagnation in oppositional thinking corresponds to his inability to progress beyond the "naive understanding" and "empirical explanation" that constitute the first stages of Ricoeur's hermeneutical arc. Because the Western tradition of empiricism depends heavily on such oppositions, John's stagnation is not accidental and suggests Irving's oblique commentary on the benighted narrowness of such reliance.

Ricoeur argues that in the final stage of the hermeneutical arc the interpreter not only discovers a more comprehensive meaning of a text but undergoes a profound personal transformation. In this "hermeneutical moment," the interpreter combines text and self in a new contextualization: "the interrogation, transgressing the closure of the text, is carried toward . . . the sort of world opened up by it." By completing the hermeneutical circle, the interpreter finds not only the text's meaning but himself or herself: "in hermeneutical reflection . . . the constitution of the self is contemporaneous with the constitution of meaning." This process of "appropriation" (*Aneignung*) "gives the subject new capacities for knowing himself" and replaces the "narcissistic ego" with "a self."

Whereas John abjectly fails to achieve such fruition, Owen clearly does. At first one might argue that Owen represents the danger of over-reliance on faith, since his faith in fulfilling his destiny and serving God lead to his early death. This is close to Hester's view, biased as she is toward keeping him alive. Yet Owen does achieve Ricoeur's third phase of enlightened understanding. He moves beyond initial guessing at meanings, works through a long period of empirical explanation, and then demonstrates his acquisition of an integrated self through his composure, his self-confidence, his eager acceptance of his responsibilities once that destiny becomes clear to him, and his sense of what William James calls an "ecstasy of happiness" as he completes that destiny.

Owen's experience corresponds not only to Ricoeur's hermeneutical arc but also to James's criteria of religious experience: a sense of certainty; a sense of perceiving new truths; "an immediate elation and freedom, as the outlines of the confining selfhood melt down"; a shift from an emotional "no" to an emotional "yes." For Owen, as for James's mystic, the authority of rationalistic consciousness collapses, replaced by his "affective experience" and his sense of union with the spiritual universe. His actions and words, his life, become inseparable from his perceived mission to save the lives of Johnny and the Vietnamese children.

John Irving and John Wheelwright shape the narrative so that it culminates in the lengthy account of Owen's heroic death in a temporary restroom in the Phoenix airport. The climax occurs when Johnny lifts Owen to the windowsill, a reiteration of "the shot" which the two boys had practiced endlessly on a basketball court, so that Owen can smother Dick Jarvits's grenade, thus saving the Vietnamese children, the nuns and Johnny, but killing himself. In that account, all the novel's motifs come together, such as Owen's commanding voice and leadership, armlessness, the debilitating effects of the Vietnam War on America, and Owen's possible divinity. On the one hand, the account reflects John's overblown sentimentality for Owen and his clearly biased claims of Owen's divinity and foreknowledge of events. On the other hand, the account, especially of Owen's death and subsequent ascent, will inspire even the most skeptical:

> We did not realize that there were forces beyond our play. Now I know they were the forces that contributed to our illusion of Owen's weightlessness; they were the forces we didn't have the faith to feel, they were the forces we failed to believe in—and they were also lifting up Owen Meany, taking him out of our hands.

Irving seems to have it both ways: he pressures readers to be wary of over-reliance on any principle, any abstraction, any target of interpretation, any article of faith or any method of knowing—no matter how noble sounding, intriguing or persuasive. Yet, having debunked all such notions, Irving nevertheless demonstrates the power of transcendent faith. Readers are led to doubt, yet they are moved.

Like Ricoeur, Irving seems to validate the "highly mediated dialectic" between "explanation" and "understanding" and to discredit reliance on any single, fixed approach. Yet, whereas Owen's apparent fulfillment underscores the power of this mediation, John Wheelwright's sterile rigidity calls it into question. Irving not only problematizes any reliance on any single position, but he further creates doubts about the efficacy of Ricoeur's dialectic. By offering and simultaneously questioning supposedly contrasting ways of knowing, and similarly by debunking traditional polarities between genders and conventional presuppositions about narratives, Irving's parodic approach implies that no single position is sufficient, that even the dialectic embrace of both positions is suspect, and that instead we must rely on the play between and among a confusing but wondrous array of possibilities.

TODD F. DAVIS AND KENNETH WOMACK

Saints, Sinners and the Dickensian Novel: The Ethics of Storytelling in John Irving's The Cider House Rules

> The intention of a novel by Charles Dickens is to move you emotionally, not intellectually; and it is by emotional means that Dickens intends to influence you socially.
> —*John Irving, "The King of the Novel"*

In addition to affording readers the critical machinery for exploring the nature of concepts such as community, stylistics, and goodness in narratives, ethical criticism provides us with a useful rhetoric for examining the function of storytelling in literary works. The act of narration—or what Adam Zachary Newton refers to in *Narrative Ethics* (1995) as the "performative function of storytelling"—can itself offer significant insight into the ethical properties of a given text. Ethical criticism presupposes that through their depictions of so many morally disparate heroes and villains, works of art necessarily implore us to render value judgments based upon our experiences as readers and members of the larger human community. Yet the act of storytelling—the manner in which writers deliberately construct their narratives so as to register moral or social impacts upon their readers—remains largely unexamined in the considerable and growing literature devoted to the interpretive mode of ethical criticism. In *Story Line: Exploring the Literature of the Appalachian Trail* (1998), Ian Marshall notes that literary criticism's purpose

From *Style: Family Systems Psychotherapy and Literature/Literary Criticism* 32, no. 2 (August 1998). © 1998 by *Style*.

"is not simply to help us understand literature but to help us understand our lives, and sometimes our lives and the literature we read help us understand critical theories." Marshall's observation about the reflexivity of literary criticism underscores one of ethical criticism's principal functions: to provide readers not only with a mechanism for comprehending the vicissitudes of human experience, but also with the interpretive tools for recognizing the ways in which writers create meaning through storytelling.

In *Cultivating Humanity: A Classical Defense of Reform in Liberal Education* (1997), Martha C. Nussbaum reminds us that "a central role of art is to challenge conventional wisdom and values." In his novels, John Irving continues to experiment with a narrative voice that seeks to thwart deliberately his readers' expectations, to upset our notions of conventionality, and to blur the boundaries that linger between good and evil, right and wrong. From the life-affirming presence of the "good, smart bears" in *The Hotel New Hampshire* (1981) and Owen Meany's shrill voice of reason in *A Prayer for Owen Meany* (1989) to the convoluted sexual politics of *The 158-Pound Marriage* (1974) and the conspicuous proximity of the "Under Toad" and the tragedy of the Ellen Jamesians in *The World According to Garp* (1978), Irving adorns his fictions with a host of ethical signifiers that challenge readers at every turn throughout his labyrinthine, deliberately Dickensian fictions. Irving makes little secret of his affinity for Dickens and in particular for the Victorian writer's eye for complexity of narrative and literary character. In "King of the Novels," Irving writes that "Dickens was abundant and magnificent with description, with the atmosphere surrounding everything—and with the tactile, with every detail that was terrifying or viscerally felt." As with Dickens, because Irving loads his own narratives with considerable detail and description, he makes it virtually impossible for readers to render facile ethical decisions in the face of so much information about a given character's humanity. Irving self-consciously adopts the literary form of the Dickensian novel—with its multiplicity of characters, its narrative mass, its overt sense of sentimentality, and its generic intersections with such modes as the detective story—as the forum for constructing the fictions that intentionally challenge his readers' value systems. In short, for Irving the choice of the narrative form of the Dickensian novel itself represents an ethical move.

The essential formulation of the Dickensian novel as a narrative form finds its origins in Dickens's dynamic approach to literary character. In *Poetic Justice: The Literary Imagination and Public Life* (1995), Nussbaum remarks that Dickens endows his characters with "physical and moral attributes that make it possible for us to distinguish every one from every other. We are made to attend to their ways of moving and talking, the shapes of their bodies, the expressions on their faces, the sentiments of their hearts. The inner life of each is displayed as having psychological depth and complexity," she adds, and "we see that as humans they share certain common problems and common hopes." Yet Dickens's characters are far more than mere vessels of transport for the essential elements of genuine human behavior. The effectiveness of Dickens's characters as human representations lies in their peculiar lack of ethical certainty, in their capacity for mimicking the elusive qualities that often define human nature. Dickens's "characters do not so much recreate actual individuals as re-create the reactions to actual individuals, and particularly the difficulties and dilemmas," Brian Rosenberg writes in *Little Dorrit's Shadows: Character and Contradiction in Dickens* (1996); "his doubts about the potential for understanding others capture a nearly universal uncertainty, and his struggle to make sense of conflicting, unreliable pieces of information mirrors a struggle we undergo daily. Shunning the rounded and definite, he leaves the reader," Rosenberg continues, "like many of the figures in his novels, always contending with the elusive and irreconcilable."

As a literary model, the Dickensian novel provides the narrative structure for Irving's own ethics of storytelling. In *The Cider House Rules* (1985), Irving avails himself of many of the Dickensian form's classic narratological elements, including its intentionally conflicted melange of characters, its intricate layering of plots, its penchant for the detective story, and even its frequent depiction of orphans, the occupants of society's most innocent and vulnerable stations. *The Cider House Rules* also affords Irving a venue for challenging our assumptions, fears, and prejudices about abortion, that most fractious of social issues. Rather than merely rendering an overt decision about the ethics of abortion, Irving, using the Dickensian mode of characterization, chooses to confront his readers with detailed, fully realized visions of the complications and uncertainties that comprise the human condition. Despite Irving's careful and deliberately indeterminate depiction of human nature in his novel, Carol C. Harter and James R. Thompson argue that as a polemic *The Cider House Rules* "is seriously flawed," and because "Irving's 'correct political vision' sometimes distorts the book's larger theme—the problematical nature of personal and social 'rules'—the difficulties with Irving's new fiction are considerable." Yet Harter and Thompson's critique of *The Cider House Rules* neglects to allow for the tremendous import of Irving's ethics of storytelling in the novel. As an essentially Dickensian novelist, Irving simply refuses to permit his readers to resort to easy and obvious decisions about either his own ethos or the ethical systems of his characters. With its variegated landscape of humanity—and the elusiveness and uncertainty that genuine humanity necessarily entails—the Dickensian novel functions in *The Cider House Rules* as the ethical vehicle via which Irving challenges his readers to consider the abortion debate from a host of vantage points, rather than merely adopting a "correct political vision."

In *Ethics, Evil and Fiction* (1997), Colin McGinn writes that "the fictional world is really the ideal world in which to go on ethical expeditions: it is safe, convenient, inconsequential, and expressly designed for our exploration and delight." Irving's own approach to storytelling—his technique, as well as his understanding of its purposes—demonstrates the ethical force of the narrative act as he conceives it. "Art has an aesthetic responsibility to be entertaining," Irving argues. "The writer's responsibility is to take hard stuff and make it as accessible as the stuff can be made." In contrast to the contemporary direction of much poststructuralist literary criticism, however, Irving does not mean to suggest that those narratives that entertain are somehow less serious or less ethically challenging. On the contrary—as Dickens's Victorian-era canon and Irving's late twentieth-century oeuvre seem to demonstrate—to entertain one's readers is to capture their hearts and minds in such a way that draws them into the lives of characters who populate stories that truly matter within the larger narrative of our shared humanity. "John Irving belongs to a small group of American writers," Terrence Des Pres suggests in *Writing into the Worm* (1991), "whose work has inspired respect for the plainest of reasons—these people write a kind of fiction useful, as genuine art must always be useful, to spiritual need." In his attempt to entertain and enlighten readers, as Irving creates texts rich with the vibrancy and contrariness of existence, he portrays not only our "spiritual need" but also ways of coping with that need. In fact, the very form of Irving's storytelling seems to suggest a means for coping spiritually, for it offers a process that brings no final answers but invites us to take part in an unforgettable journey. As he tells his story, Irving moves his readers beyond the present moment in the text into a deep history of both the characters in the story and the communities in which they live; he compels his readers to wrestle with the same ethical dilemmas that the story's characters must confront; he causes us to see and feel the joy, anger, and sorrow that inevitably visits itself upon the saints and sinners who populate the landscape of his fiction. Like the wrestler he was—indeed, he is—Irving deliberately weaves his tales into the emotional lives of his readers. Snaking his characters' arms and legs around one another, he leaves us in the most improbable and compromising positions: entwined on the mat of his story, struggling not to be pinned by the weight of the lives we enter vicariously.

How, then, does Irving achieve this kind of connection with his readers, and why do the characters within Irving's fictional world remain vivid in the minds of both his devoted popular readership and the literati? Writing against the grain of much contemporary artistic practice, Irving grounds his achievement in his use of the particular and his consistent desire for the subject of his fictions to be recognizable in the world beyond the text. In his published interviews and memoirs, Irving laments the shift in contemporary fiction away from the actual world in which we live toward the world of metafiction. In a 1979 interview, Irving addresses the debate taking place during that era between John Gardner and William Gass about the "necessity or irrelevancy of art's allegiance to morality": "Gardner has been very careless about a number of things he's said, so it's easier to pick on Gardner than it is to pick on Gass," Irving explains; "on the other hand, it seems to me that Gardner has tried to say a lot more about literature than Gass, and I have to admire him for that. I'd also have to agree with Gardner that literature should be a sign of life rather than a celebration of death," Irving concludes, "and if a novel doesn't address itself to something of human value, I don't see much worth in it." Irving's insistence that the novel as literary form should address "something of human value" continues to determine many of his narrative practices, especially his use of the particular. By chronicling several major and minor characters' histories in his novels with an uncanny precision and attentiveness, Irving creates an ethical construct that for the purposes of this essay we shall refer to as "characterscape."

While novelists must in some manner establish character for their readers, not all writers agree about its import or the techniques necessary to produce it. In *Find You the Virtue: Ethics, Image, and Desire in Literature* (1987), Irving Massey contends that the ethics of particularity, the ability to see the individual rather than the universal, illustrates the folly in ideas of repetition and categorization: "Things just do not repeat themselves, unless we are passive to them: if they exist for us fully, we do not experience them under the aspect of sameness or uniformity. Categories have something of the fraud about them." The ability to see human events and experiences for what they are, to be fully attentive to their originality, is a central concept in Irving's creation of characterscape. In order to understand more fully the notion of characterscape, it should be noted that this construct does not differ significantly from the creation of character in terms of technique, but it does differ radically in terms of intention. As with the creation of character, characterscape requires the description of specific incidents that reflect the inner life of a given character's personhood; fundamental elements of anatomy, dress, physical movements, professional habits, and the like must be foregrounded for readers. In contrast with mere characterization, however, characterscape operates upon a scale of grand proportion. This is not to say that a given character is necessarily grandiose or ethical in his or her own right; on the contrary, in *The Cider House Rules* Irving borrows from Dickens by making an orphan of diminutive and humble stature a central figure in the action of his novel. Instead, the concept of proportion relates to the amount of narrative space used to create a vivid rendering of a particular character. This process might best be compared to William Least Heat-Moon's appropriation of landscape in *PrairyErth: A Deep Map* (1991). The subtitle of Heat-Moon's opus underscores the issue at hand: we must examine what lies within the deeper structures of the worlds that we inhabit to understand fully what lives before our eyes. By probing beneath the surface of Chase County, Kansas, and viewing it from nearly every imaginable position, Heat-Moon confronts his readers with a mental image that transcends landscape; it is as if the writer has found a way not only to transform the two-dimensional art of words on the printed page into a three-dimensional representation, but also has discovered a vehicle to transport readers into other dimensions that fuse the physical and the spiritual, the animal and the human into a single landscape.

As with Heat-Moon's work of creative nonfiction, Irving's fictional-world characterscapes offer multidimensional perspectives. Certainly, *The Cider House Rules* might be told more succinctly if we were not presented first with the history of St. Cloud's—including such ephemeral facts as how the town's name acquired an apostrophe—and then with the history of Wilbur Larch and his circuitous journey into medicine and the practice of abortion. Yet if such material were excised, the novel's range would be radically truncated and Larch's complicated motivations for performing abortions would not be fully realized. Characterscape demands that many of the issues and incidents to which we are not privy in our workaday lives beyond the confines of the text—specially such wonderful artifice as *The Cider House Rules*'s epilogue that permits us not only to see the past, but also the past in the context of the future—be presented in such a way that our understanding of the fictional persons that we encounter as we consume the story expands voluminously toward an ethical illumination of far-reaching consequence. Of course, not all readers will accept the invitation to enter fully into Irving's fictive world, but because of its narrative mass the sheer number of hours that such storytelling requires makes possible this kind of revelatory relationship.

By carefully and expansively layering his presentation of character, Irving satisfies his own demand that philosophical issues be subservient to the ways in which people live. Characterscape functions as Irving's central ethic: the physical world of human activity—which he attempts to make as vibrantly alive as possible—must never be lost in a philosophical debate about notions of right and wrong. As with William Carlos Williams, Irving dismisses the abstract and embraces the physical. In *The Call of Stories: Teaching and the Moral Imagination* (1989), Robert Coles explains that

Williams's "repeated call to arms, the well-known phrase 'no ideas but in things,' is a prelude to distinctions he kept making between poetry and life; between ideas and action; between the abstract and the concrete; between theory and practice; and not least, between art and conduct." In similar fashion, Irving also proclaims adamantly that fiction must originate in the concrete and the physical as opposed to the philosophical, and he offers a litany of complaints against those novels that seem more about a particular ideology than about the lives that transpire within a given text: "I guess another way to put this," explains Irving, "is that I don't like to see a thesis about life, or people, disguised as a novel. I don't think the greatest novels of our time or any other time are theses. Great novels succeed much better when they are broad expressions or portraits than when they confine themselves to the singularity of an idea."

Although *The Cider House Rules* has been both criticized and lauded as an "idea" book, one that crusades for a singular position on the abortion issue, we would do well to note the author's own account of the novel's genesis: "I wanted to write an orphan novel. It was a year before abortion entered the story," Irving remarks, "but it made perfect sense. In the early part of the century, what doctor would be most sympathetic to performing abortions but a doctor who delivered unwanted babies, then cared for them in an orphanage?" Repeating his litany in an interview with Alison Freeland—"a novel is not single-issue politics, or if it is, it's not a novel"—Irving derides those critics who read *The Cider House Rules* in terms of a single political vision. This narrowness of vision, of course, demonstrates precisely the problem with Harter and Thompson's critique of the novel as "polemic." While Irving admits that *The Cider House Rules* is perhaps his first polemical novel, Harter and Thompson's understanding of Irving's use of the polemic fails to account for the significance of the characterscapes that undergird Irving's fictions. Undoubtedly, Irving proffers a novel that sets forth an argument of great controversy, but, as is his practice elsewhere, the lives of his characters and the events that transpire remain too broad and various to represent a single, essentialist position within the abortion debate. Irving's confession that the novel has a polemic quality merely asserts the reality that the historic stage upon which his players strut has for its backdrop an orphanage where, in the words of Larch, some babies and some mothers are "delivered." Arguing that this notion functions as the political vision of the novel neglects the character motivations and histories of both Wilbur Larch and Homer Wells. While Larch indeed crusades in covert and overt ways for the right of women to choose, he remains in the novel but one character among many whose past seems to compromise his ideological position in the present. The same may be said of Homer as he grapples with his role in performing abortions, as well as of the many different women who receive abortions during the course of the novel and their markedly different motivations for seeking out such a dramatic and final solution. In his review of *The Cider House Rules*, Benjamin DeMott contends that the value of Irving's novel lies in its treatment of abortion as a subject rooted both in our collective past and in the heterogeneous ways in which we live in the present. Irving's approach to this subject actually demonstrates the impossibility of rendering a facile ethical decision when confronted with such a divisive issue. In "an age ill at ease with the notion that art can have a subject," DeMott praises Irving for his awareness of human relationships where abstract philosophies and political ideologies play themselves out. "Irving draws the readers close in the space of his imagination," says DeMott, "to an understanding of essential links, commonalties—even unities—between factions now seething with hatred for each other."

For this reason, Irving focuses significant time and energy upon narrating intricate accounts of numerous characters' lives. In *The Cider House Rules*, Irving offers detailed histories not only of the novel's two main characters, Wilbur Larch and Homer Wells, but also of Melony, Wally Worthington, and Candy Kendall, among others. In "The King of the Novel," John Irving observes that "you cannot encounter the prisons in Dickens's novels and ever again feel completely self-righteous about prisoners being where they belong; you cannot encounter a lawyer of Mr. Jaggers's terrifying ambiguity and ever again put yourself willingly in a lawyer's hands—Jaggers, although only a minor character in *Great Expectations*, may be our literature's greatest indictment of living by abstract rules." The same might be said of Irving's own depiction of abortion and the figure of Wilbur Larch, obstetrician and abortionist, in *The Cider House Rules*. Like Dickens, Irving derides the notion of living by abstract rules, and in the person of Larch he begins his assault upon the "rules" that govern the concept of abortion.

Although his associates at the orphanage refer to him as St. Larch, Irving makes perfectly clear that Larch's sainthood comes with a price. Upon Larch's admission to and imminent departure for medical school, Larch's father purchases for Wilbur an evening with a local prostitute, Mrs. Eames. This rather embarrassing evening of sexual initiation concludes with Wilbur dressing in the glow of a cigar being smoked by Mrs. Eames's daughter, who enters unannounced while Wilbur drowses in post-coital bliss. What Larch seems to take from this experience—in addition to gonorrhea, which he studies in bacteriology at Harvard Medical School—is a substantial measure of remorse. Wilbur compounds his guilty conscience through a series of events that bring Mrs. Eames and her daughter back into his life. While working as a young intern at the South End Branch of the Boston Lying-In, Larch treats Mrs. Eames, whom he discovers has been taking an aborticide that leaves her organs in a state of "fragile jelly." After six days of Larch's care, Mrs. Eames dies, and in the ensuing autopsy Larch learns from the pathologist that she has expired as a result of scurvy. A day later, as only happens in the fabulistic world of Dickens and Irving, where coincidences are indispensable to the connective tissue of characterscape, Mrs. Eames's daughter visits Larch. She shows him the aborticide that her mother ingested—a "French Lunar Solution" said to restore "Female Monthly Regularity!"—and asks him to perform an abortion for her: "I ain't quick! I ain't quick, I said!" she screams at Larch. But the consequences of the proce-dure frighten Lurch and he hesitates. A week later Larch finds her beaten and in grave condition after receiving an abortion at the shady clinic known only as "Off Harrison." He discovers a note pinned to her battered body: "DOCTOR LARCH—SHIT OR GET OFF THE POT!" As with her mother only days before, Mrs. Eames's daughter also dies in the care of Larch, but her death prompts him to visit "Off Harrison" and confront the abortionist who runs the clinic, an elderly woman known locally as Mrs. Santa Claus. This scene allows readers to see the tools of abortion, and, along with Larch, to be shocked by the awful conditions and misguided methods under which illegal abortions are conducted. This experience also serves as the catalyst for Larch's ultimate role as abortionist in the novel. In short, the kinds of metaphorical gifts that Mrs. Claus delivers challenge Larch to seek a practical and immediate solution for such women in need as Mrs. Eames and her daughter—a solution generated out of the pragmatics of physical circumstance as opposed to legalistic ideology.

With each horrific incident, Irving adds one more layer to Larch's characterscape, but, in so doing, Irving refuses to render any overt value judgments and offers nothing more than the precarious elements of human storytelling. Although abortion clearly lies at the center of these passages, Irving carefully avoids entering into a philosophical debate about when life actually begins or whose rights must be protected. Irving eschews any theo-logical discussion that might affect the actions of his characters or the manner in which readers might interpret those actions. Interestingly, Larch's decision seems to spring from his understanding of his own fallibility, his own fallen nature. Through his interaction with Mrs. Eames and her daughter he recognizes the culpability of his own conduct, as well as that of a society that tacitly condones the creation of orphans, prostitutes, and unwanted pregnancies. In a particularly telling moment of reflection, Larch contemplates the peculiar interrelationship between celibacy and moral condemnation:

On his mind was Mrs. Eames's daughter's last puff of cigar breath in his face as he bent over her before she died—reminding him, of course, of the night he needed her puffing cigar to find his clothes. If pride was a sin, thought Dr. Larch, the greatest sin was moral pride. He had slept with someone's mother and dressed himself in the light of her daughter's cigar. He could quite comfortably abstain from having sex for the rest of his life, but how could he ever condemn another person for having sex?

Larch's unspoken vow of celibacy and his assumption of sainthood, like the disorderly nature of all genuinely human activity, finds its roots in interpersonal relationships, and in his relationships with women, Larch continually falters. As with his addiction to ether—which begins as a practical remedy to the gonorrhea he contracts from Mrs. Eames and later becomes a means for both relaxing and, perhaps, escaping temporarily from his guilt—his response to abortion represents the actions of a pragmatic doctor doing the practical things necessary for his patients and the community in which he lives. After denying Mrs. Eames's daughter an abortion, he never again pauses to consider the legal or ethical ramifications of abortion when faced with a mother in need. Instead, as Larch explains in *A Brief History of St. Cloud's*, "Here in St. Cloud's we would waste our limited energy and our limited imagination by regarding the sordid facts of life as if they were problems." For Larch, pragmatism reigns; because the "sordid facts of life" can never be changed, one's moral position must never be lorded over the physical needs of another. Later within the very same chapter, "The Lord's Work," in which he offers his first pronouncement of celibacy and his confession that moral pride amounts to the worst of sins, Larch reaffirms this notion in the precise language of the earlier passage. In this manner, the saint of both orphans and mothers establishes a mantra that allows him to carry on with his duties:

> Later, when he would have occasion to doubt himself, he would force himself to remember: he had slept with someone's mother and dressed himself in the light of her daughter's cigar. He could quite comfortably abstain from having sex for the rest of his life, but how could he ever condemn another person for having sex? He would remember, too, what he hadn't done for Mrs. Eames's daughter, and what that had cost.
> He would deliver babies. He would deliver mothers, too.

Yet the most significant test of Larch's resolve comes not with the first abortion he performs for the young girl he rescues from "Off Harrison" or the subsequent requests by others in the neighborhood community who find themselves in similar straits, but from a wealthy family, the Channing-Peabodys of Boston, who summer in Portland, Maine. Larch has gone to Maine to apply for a position in obstetrics, escaping Boston where he "had become, in the view of the erring, the sanctuary to which to flee." Larch ostensibly visits the Channing-Peabodys's palatial mansion for what he assumes will be a dinner party. Neither poor nor downtrodden like the women who sought out Larch in South Boston, the Channing-Peabodys prove insufferable in their moral superiority and in their presumption that their money can relieve them of any set of unpleasant or undesired circumstances. Despite such arrogance, Larch still cannot bring himself to pass judgment upon Missy, the woman in need of his services. Instead of refusing the Channing-Peabodys, he insists that the young man responsible for impregnating Missy be sent in to watch the procedure—and, as Larch hopes, the young man vomits all over himself. Additionally, taking the money with which the Channing-Peabodys attempt to "buy" his services and his silence, Larch chooses to distribute it among the servants who help him perform the abortion, as well as among those others who work throughout the great house. Such a scene, particularly important in the creation of Larch's own characterscape, demonstrates his ethical determination to refuse to judge the woman in need of his care. While Larch indeed passes judgment upon those characters who seem to stand in supposed moral superiority over Missy for becoming pregnant and over him for becoming a doctor who would perform abortions, he will not deny any woman, in this instance Missy, whom he clearly sees as a victim.

By availing himself of the ethos of characterscape, Irving establishes the motivations and the ideology of Larch, a man who claims to do both "the Lord's work and the Devil's work." He further complicates our understanding of Larch as both saint and sinner by introducing the figure of Homer Wells, the eternal orphan who becomes a surrogate son for Larch, as well as his professional successor. Homer's presence in the frame of Irving's story exemplifies the ethics of characterscape by illustrating the marked importance of human interrelationships in the construction of characterscape. Just as a landscape artist needs a horizon and a sky, a foreground and a background to capture properly the spirit of a place, the writer who hopes to achieve a fully articulated portrait of a character must place the person in close relation to another character of consequence within a given narrative. While Irving devotes the bulk of *The Cider House Rules*'s narrative space to Homer's story, the orphan would not achieve his full semblance of personhood without the character of Larch to bring him into bas-relief.

As the boy whose adoption never comes to pass, Homer undergoes a trial by fire of sorts that consists of several horribly fantastic adoptive experiences, including in one instance his "buggering" by a sibling and in another case the death of his new parents in a thunderous rushing flood of logs and water on a camping expedition. As he inevitably returns to St. Cloud's, he develops a special relationship, unique and full of mutual love, with Larch. Because Homer grows to the age of "usefulness," as Larch calls it, while still residing at St. Cloud's, Larch initiates him into the world of the orphanage, first as a caregiver and later as an obstetrician. For example, Larch assigns Homer the nightly task of reading works by Dickens and Brontë to the orphans in both the girls' and boys' divisions. In this capacity, Homer develops a relationship with another "older" orphan, Melony, who, like himself, has yet to be adopted successfully. Melony functions as the first female character to affect Homer's understanding of the world of sexuality and trust. As with Larch, Homer's feelings about abortion, sex, and procreation become fundamentally altered by his relations with women. In the Dickensian tradition of the detective story, Melony's character provides Irving with the means for availing himself of the generic conventions of the detective mode to trace one of the principal desires of many orphans: to know the identity of their parents and to know who loves them. Melony's menacing attitude toward her undiscovered parents, as well as her promise to Homer that she will perform fellatio upon him if he locates the records of her parents' identity in Larch's office, inaugurates the quirky commitment that exists between Melony and Homer. Although her first investigation as Irving's *de facto* detective fails because Larch makes it a practice not to maintain adoption records, Melony searches for love in the person of Homer, whom she coerces into a promise that, in the fleeting world of St. Cloud's, must inevitably be broken:

> "If I stay, you'll stay—is that what you're saying?" Melony asked him. Is that what I mean? thought Homer Wells. But Melony, as usual, gave him no time to think. "Promise me you'll stay as long as I stay, Sunshine," Melony said. She moved closer to him; she took his hand and opened his fingers and put his index finger in her mouth.

While Homer and Melony develop a sexual relationship, even a loving relationship of sorts, Homer ultimately breaks his commitment to Melony when he goes to live at Heart's Rock upon the invitation of Wally Worthington and Candy Kendall.

Irving later reintroduces the Dickensian detective story after Melony searches for Homer and finally confronts him in the Worthingtons' orchard. In addition to immediately recognizing Angel as Homer and Candy's son,

Irving's orphan *cum* detective later succeeds in finding Homer, despite her untimely death, when her cadaver tracks Homer to St. Cloud's and metaphorically unravels his secret identity as Dr. F. Stone. While Irving employs the detective mode to entertain his readers with suspense—as with the detective story that undergirds the latter third of his most recent novel, *A Widow for One Year* (1998)—the ethics of storytelling insists that Irving employ Melony's investigation to establish a layer in Homer's characterscape that will eventually contribute to his return to St. Cloud's as Larch's replacement. While Melony's detective tale allows Irving to establish the gravity of Homer's betrayal of her, as well as that of his subsequent betrayal of Wally Worthington, it also affects the manner in which he sees the "sins" of others. As with Larch's convoluted relationships with women in *The Cider House Rules*, Homer's broken promise to Melony and his secret love for Candy teach him to see life's variegated shades of meaning, to understand the foibles of human interaction, and to recognize that a legalistic approach to "rules" never reveals the full complexity of any situation.

Yet for Homer such a lesson comes slowly. To this end, Irving offers three extraordinary scenes that demonstrate Homer's exceptional compassion, his devotion to the delivery of babies and their mothers. The first encounter takes place when Homer is relatively young but old enough to have been instructed by Larch to be of some "use." Because of orphan Fuzzy Stone's coughing and the noise the machines make that help Fuzzy breathe, on certain nights Homer roams the halls of the orphanage, often seeking out the baby room or the mothers' room. On this particular night, while standing in the mothers' room, a mysterious pregnant woman asks Homer if he would, at his age, leave the orphanage with a family who wishes to adopt him. He replies that he would not. Of course, the woman asks this question because she wants to be reassured that her baby will find an adoptive home and be cared for in ways she cannot offer. Homer does not sense this at first, however, and despite several attempts on the mother's part to elicit a "yes" from Homer, he seems fixed in his opinion that St. Cloud's is the only home he will ever know. The mother begins to cry and asks Homer if he wishes to be of "use" and touch her pregnant belly:

> "No one but me ever put a hand on me, to feel that baby. No one wanted to put his ear against it and listen," the woman said. "You shouldn't have a baby if there's no one who wants to feel it kick, or listen to it move."

The woman asks Homer again if he wishes to be of use and suggests that he "sleep right here" where the baby rests beneath her stomach. Homer feigns sleep until the woman's water breaks. After the birth of the child, Homer plays a game with himself. Because of his "nighttime vigil with his face upon the mother's jumping belly" he hopes to recognize her child. This incident profoundly affects the way Homer looks at not only the women who come to St. Cloud's to be delivered of some of their problems—"Importantly, Homer knew they did not look delivered of all their problems when they left. No one he had seen looked more miserable than those women"—but also the way that he looks at their pregnant bellies, the potential lives that will either be aborted or delivered by the hands of St. Larch. Because of his sympathetic vigil upon the belly of this mother, Homer cannot bring himself to believe what Larch preaches about abortion. At the same time, because of his relationship with Larch he cannot condemn his "father's" actions either.

Shortly before his departure to Heart's Rock, Homer experiences an epiphany of sorts about his own right to choose what he will believe regarding abortion. In this second scene, Homer examines a fetus that bled to death during a failed delivery performed by Latch:

> Homer felt there was nothing as simple as anyone's fault involved; it was not Larch's fault—Larch did what he believed in. If Wilbur Larch was a saint to Nurse Angela and to Nurse Edna, he was both a saint and a father to Homer Wells. Larch knew what he was doing—and for whom. But that quick and not-quick stuff: it didn't work for Homer Wells. You can call it a fetus, or an embryo, or the products of conception, thought Homer Wells, but whatever you call it, it's alive. And whatever you do to it, Homer thought—and whatever you call what you do—you're killing it, [. . .] Let Larch call it whatever he wants, thought Homer Wells. It's his choice—if it's a fetus, to him, that's fine. It's a baby to me, thought Homer Wells. If Larch has a choice, I have a choice, too.

Later at Heart's Rock, after Candy becomes pregnant and mentions a trip to St. Cloud's for a possible abortion, Homer—motivated by his intense convictions about the sanctity of human life—tells her that "it's my baby, too," that he also bears responsibility for the life that they created together and in which he wishes to participate. Unlike Larch, who in his later years withdraws more deeply into his ether addiction and his medical routine because he believes that "love was certainly not safe—not ever," Homer self-consciously shares his love with others and cannot imagine a life without Candy or his newly conceived baby. Because he believes that Wally died in the war, Homer avoids confronting his guilt over the love he has shared with

Candy or his betrayal of his best friend. Soon after the birth of Angel—baptized symbolically by a drop of Larch's sweat as he delivers him—the news that Wally has been found alive tests Homer's love for Candy, Wally, and Angel. Yet Homer's real challenge comes fifteen years later, shortly after the death of Larch by an accidental ether overdose.

In the third scene, Irving—using relational characterscape in conjunction with the Dickensian grand style of convergence—assembles all of the characters who have affected Homer's life most profoundly. In the novel's final chapter, aptly entitled "Breaking the Rules," Homer faces multiple, nearly simultaneous decisions regarding various "rules" of ethical behavior. The impact of these decisions upon those characters that he loves and lives with make these issues especially difficult. As the title of the chapter intimates, Homer will "break the rules," and, in so doing, he will come to understand that ethical law cannot be approached legalistically, a point that Irving underscores via his own method of storytelling. While certain rules once governed Homer's silence about his love for Candy and their true relationship to one another and their son Angel, in the end Homer recognizes—courtesy of Melony's recognition of the child's lineage—that the truth must be told. Similarly, such remarkably human situations force Homer to contemplate the possibility that certain abstract rules cannot be reconciled with the practical, physical needs of the moment, that human suffering cannot be judged or sacrificed to legalism. As the foreman of the orchard for the last fifteen years, moreover, Homer bears the responsibility for posting "the cider house rules." At times, the fact that the work crew does not follow the rules bothers Homer. In a conversation with Mr. Rose, however, Homer begins to realize that the ways in which people live together in human community actually govern the "rules"; those rules established by forces outside the community cannot produce this same effect. Mr. Rose explains, for example, that within the black community of migrant workers who live at the orchard during harvest there emerge unwritten rules engendered from human relationships that have nothing to do with Homer's rules. Yet Homer cannot bring himself fully to accept the relational as well as contextual aspects of ethical rules; he finds it difficult to comprehend that those rules imposed from without "never asked" but "told"—a fact that itself explains the ineffectiveness of legalistic codes in contrast with ethical rules.

Ultimately, Homer's decision to perform an abortion for Rose Rose, Mr. Rose's pregnant daughter and Angel's first love, alters his perspective about the procedure, but Homer does not reach this decision easily. A few weeks before Rose Rose's crisis, Homer writes to Larch in order to refuse his invitation to come to St. Cloud's and replace St. Larch in the operation of the orphanage. As he writes in his laconic, numbered letter to Larch:

1. I AM NOT A DOCTOR. 2. I BELIEVE THE FETUS HAS A SOUL. 3. I'M SORRY.

In short, Homer refuses to break the "rules" that govern the practice of medicine. He also feels that he cannot perform an abortion because of an ethical belief in the sanctity of the human soul. At the same time, he regrets these decisions because of his loyalty and love for his "father," St. Larch. While both his belief in the sanctity of the human soul and his conviction that the fetus is fully human remain static, Homer, when faced with Larch's untimely death and his own status as the only person available to perform a safe abortion on Rose Rose, simply cannot refuse his patient's wish to abort her pregnancy. Although Irving depicts Homer's first abortion as representative of the most extreme and awful form of conception—Rose Rose has been impregnated by her own father, breaking all of the rules—Homer nevertheless believes as strongly in the sanctity of Rose Rose's fetus as he would in the sanctity of any other fetus conceived under less ethically challenging circumstances. As he confesses to Candy, Homer finds abortion problematic, for he considers it tantamount to "killing" a human being:

> "I'm a little nervous," Homer admitted to Candy. "It's certainly not a matter of technique, and I've got everything I need—I know I can do it. It's just that, to me, it is a living human being. I can't describe to you what it feels like—just to hold the curette, for example. When living tissue is touched, it responds—somehow," Homer said, but Candy cut him off.

Homer's decision to perform the abortion illustrates the ethical imperative embodied by Irving's act of storytelling. Clearly, *The Cider House Rules* should not be read as a novel that finally embraces the act of abortion. Homer's own belief system radically contradicts such a conclusion. The novel demonstrates the conflicted nature of human dealings and the inadequacy of legalism as a means for responding to our most pressing needs. While Homer decides to assume the constructed identity that Larch invents for him—as Dr. F. Stone, a missionary obstetrician newly arrived from India—Homer recognizes that he cannot deny strangers what he would give freely to those he loves and those he knows: "Because he knew now that he couldn't play God in the worst sense; if he could operate on Rose Rose, how could he refuse to help a stranger? How could he refuse anyone? Only a god makes that kind of decision. I'll just give them what they want, he thought. An orphan or an abortion." For Homer, then, rules do not account for the fact that we are all saints and all sinners, rather than being one or the other. Legalism offers no true, compassionate, or humane answers to the abortion issue because it operates from the abstract, not from the tangible. Irving's ethics of storytelling makes all too clear that the ways our lives intersect and the impossible decisions that the business of living forces us to make cannot be handled under a single system of rules. In Irving's fictive universe—and, indeed, in our own corporeal world—only the sanctity of individual choice in relation to human community can determine the system of ethical values that governs our lives.

In this manner, Irving's appropriation of the Dickensian form establishes—especially through its use of extensive narratological and characterological detail—an ethics of particularity in which a multiperspectival history comes to bear upon our understanding of a given narrative situation. The Dickensian novel as literary mode demands that we see the ethical dimensions of the lives represented in the text as something that ethical "rules"—whether they be the rules that dictate life in a cider house or rules that govern a promise between orphans—cannot adequately address. Using the abidingly fractious issue of abortion as the background for his story of an orphanage, Irving refuses to conclude his novel with any facile statement either for or against abortion. Rather, as storyteller he insists that any genuine contemplation about the abortion issue must take place within the context of human relationships, and, as a disciple of Dickens, he paints characterscapes of such layered detail that we see the conflicted nature of human resolution. Only by providing his readership with fully realized portraits of humanity can Irving construct an adequate fictional tableau for narrating the moral dilemmas that trouble our society and the ways that we live now. As with Dickens, Irving intuitively recognizes that readers "want catharsis, they want to be stretched and tested, they want to be frightened and come through it, they want to be scared, taken out of their familiar surroundings—intellectual, visceral, spiritual—and to be reexposed to things." In *The Cider House Rules*, Irving offers precisely such an ethically complex and conflicted narrative. While some form of judgment must inevitably be rendered in the novel, clearly Homer's decision to return to St. Cloud's as Dr. F. Stone is not motivated by any "rule" about the goodness of abortion or the absolute belief that women must have a choice in the matter. As with Dr. Larch's initial decision to perform an abortion, Homer's return to St. Cloud's and all that it entails finds its origins in his genuinely human relationships with women—with Candy and Melony and Rose Rose—not out of any ideologically pure ethic. By delivering his compelling narratives and vast characterscapes through the artifice of the Dickensian novel, Irving narrates the equally captivating and convoluted stories of our own lives.

Chronology

1942   John Winslow Irving born March 2 in Exeter, New Hampshire.

1961   Graduates from Phillips Exeter Academy; enrolls at the University of Pittsburgh.

1963–64   Studies at the Institute of European Studies, University of Vienna.

1964   Marries Shyla Leary.

1965   Graduates from the University of New Hamphsire; son Colin is born.

1967   Earns Master of Fine Arts degree from the University of Iowa.

1968   First novel, *Setting Free the Bears*, is published.

1970   Son Brendan is born.

1972   Receives Rockefeller Foundation Grant; second novel, *The Water-Method Man*, is published.

1972   Begins serving as Writer-in-Residence at the Writer's Workshop, University of Iowa.

1974   *The 158-Pound Marriage* is published; receives a National Endowment of the Arts fellowship.

1975   Leaves the University of Iowa to become assistant professor of English at Mount Holyoke College.

1976   Receives a Guggenheim Foundation grant.

1978   *The World According to Garp* is published; leaves Mount Holyoke College.

1980   *The World According to Garp* wins American Book Award as best paperback novel of 1979.

1981   *The Hotel New Hampshire* is published.

1982   Obtains divorce from Shyla Leary; film version of *The World According to Garp* is released.

1985   Publishes *The Cider House Rules*.

1987   Marries Janet Turnbull.

1989   *A Prayer for Owen Meany* is published.

1991   Son Everett is born.

1993   *Trying to Save Piggy Sneed*, a collection of short stories, is published.

1994   *A Son of the Circus* is published.

1998   *A Widow for One Year* is published.

1999   Publishes a memoir, *My Movie Business*; the film version of *The Cider House Rules* wins an academy award.

Contributors

HAROLD BLOOM is Sterling Professor of the Humanities at Yale University and Henry W. and Albert A. Berg Professor of English at the New York University Graduate School. He is the author of over 20 books, including *Shelley's Mythmaking* (1959), *The Visionary Company* (1961), *Blake's Apocalypse* (1963), *Yeats* (1970), *A Map of Misreading* (1975), *Kabbalah and Criticism* (1975), *Agon: Toward a Theory of Revisionism* (1982), *The American Religion* (1992), *The Western Canon* (1994), and *Omens of Millennium: The Gnosis of Angels, Dreams, and Resurrection* (1996). *The Anxiety of Influence* (1973) sets forth Professor Bloom's provocative theory of the literary relationships between the great writers and their predecessors. His most recent books include *Shakespeare: The Invention of the Human*, a 1998 National Book Award finalist, and *How to Read and Why*, which was published in 2000. In 1999, Professor Bloom received the prestigious American Academy of Arts and Letters Gold Medal for Criticism.

GREIL MARCUS, a frequent contributor to *Rolling Stone*, is the author of *Mystery Train: Images of America in Rock 'n Roll* (1975), *Lipstick Traces: A Secret History of the 20th Century* (1989), *Dead Elvis: A Chronicle of a Cultural Obsession* (1991), and *The Dustbin of History* (1995).

BENJAMIN DeMOTT has written extensively on literary figures such as William Dean Howells, D. H. Lawrence, and E. M. Forester. He is the author of *Close Imagining: An Introduction to Literature* (1988).

MICHAEL PRIESTLY'S work has appeared in *The New York Review of Books* and in *New England Review.*

ROBERT TOWERS teaches English at Queens College. His novels include *The Necklace of Kali* (1960), *The Monkey Watcher* (1964), and *The Summoning* (1983).

JOSEPH EPSTEIN was the editor of *American Scholar*, a quarterly journal published by the Phi Beta Kappa honor society. His books include *Ambition: The Secret Passion* (1989) and *Narcissus Leaves the Pool: Familiar Essays* (1999).

GABRIEL MILLER'S works include a 1982 study of John Irving.

JANE BOWERS HILL is an instructor at the University of Georgia. She has contributed poetry to various publications, including *Kansas Quarterly*, *Cold Mountain Review*, and the *California State Poetry Quarterly*. She has also published articles on the poet James Dickey.

RAYMOND J. WILSON III teaches at Loras College in Iowa.

DEBRA SHOSTAK has written about the work of Phillip Roth, Maxine Hong Kingston, and Tim O'Brien. She is assistant professor at The College of Wooster in Ohio.

PHILIP PAGE is assistant professor of English at California State University, San Bernardino. He has published articles on Henry James, Gerard Manley Hopkins, Willa Cather, Katherine Anne Porter, and Toni Morrison.

TODD F. DAVIS has written for several journals.

KENNETH WOMACK has published articles on George Eliot, book collecting, and twentieth century western writers. He is coauthor of *Recent Works in Critical Theory, 1989–1995: An Annotated Bibliography* (1996).

Bibliography

Atlas, James. "John Irving's World." *New York Times Book Review* (13 September 1981): 1, 36, 38, 40.

Bawer, Bruce. *"The World According to Garp*: Novel to Film," in *Take Two: Adapting the Contemporary American Novel to Film,* ed. Barbara Tepa Lepak. Bowling Green, Ohio: Bowling Green State University Popular Press, 1994.

Cosgrove, William. *"The World According to Garp* as Fabulation." *South Carolina Review* 19 (Spring 1987): 52–58.

DeMott, Benjamin. "Domesticated Madness." *Atlantic Monthly* 248 (October 1981): 101–6.

Davis, Todd F., and Kenneth Womack. "Saints, Sinners and the Dickensian Novel: The Ethics of Storytelling in John Irving's *The Cider House Rules." Style: Family Systems Psychotherapy and Literature/Literary Criticism* 32, no. 2 (August 1998): 298–330.

Drabble, Marilyn. "Musk, Memory, and Imagination." *Harper's* (July 1978): 82–84.

Epstein, Joseph. "Why Is John Irving So Popular?" *Commentary* 73, no. 6 (June 1982): 59–63.

Greil, Marcus. "Garp: Death in the Family, I." *Rolling Stone* (25 August 1978): 60–63.

———. "Garp: Death in the Family, II." *Rolling Stone* (21 September 1978): 76–79.

Harter, Carol C. and James R. Thompson. *John Irving.* Boston: Twayne, 1986.

Hill, Jane Bowers. "John Irving's Aesthetics of Accessibility: Setting Free the Novel." *South Carolina Review* 16 (Fall 1983): 38–44.

Loundsberry, Barbara. "The Terrible Toad: Violence as Excessive Imagination in *The World According to Garp." Thalia* 5 (Fall/Winter 1982–83): 30–35.

Miller, Gabriel. *John Irving.* New York: Frederick Ungar, 1982.

Nelson, William. "Unlikely Heroes: The Central Figures in *The World According to Garp, Even Cowgirls Get the Blues,* and *A Confederacy of Dunces.*" In *The Hero in Transition,* ed. Ray B. Brown. Bowling Green: Bowling Green University Popular Press, 1983.

Page, Philip. "Hero Worship and Hermeneutic Dialectics: John Irving's *A Prayer for Owen Meany*." *Mosaic* 28 (September 1995): 137–156.

Priestley, Michael. "Structure in the Worlds of John Irving." *Critique: Studies in Modern Fiction* 23 (January 1981): 82–96.

Pritchard, William. *"A Prayer for Owen Meany." New Republic* (22 May 1989): 36–39.

Reilly, Edward C. *Understanding John Irving.* Columbia: University of South Carolina Press, 1991.

———. "The Anschluss and *the World According to Irving*." *Research Studies* 51 (June 1983): 98–110.

———. "John Irving's *The Hotel New Hampshire* and the Allegory of Sorrow." *Publications of the Arkansas Philological Association* 6 (Spring 1983): 78–83.

Rockwood, Bruce L., and Roberta Kevelson, eds. "Abortion Stories and Uncivil Discourse," in *Law and Literature Perspectives.* New York: Peter Lang, 1996.

Shostak, Debra. "The Family Romances of John Irving." *Essays in Literature* 21 (1994): 129–45.

Suplee, Curt. "John Irving and the Tyranny of Imagination." *Washington Post* (25 August 1981): B1, B8–9.

Sweet, Ellen. "Men Who've Taken Chances and Made a Difference." *Ms.* (July/August 1982): 102–4.

Thompson, Christine E. "Pentheus in *The World According to Garp*." *Classical and Modern Literature* 3 (Fall 1982): 33–37.

Towers, Robert. "Reservations." *New York Review of Books* 28 (5 November 1981): 12–14.

Wilson, Raymond III. "The Postmodern Novel: The Example of John Irving's *The World According to Garp*." *Critique: Studies in Modern Fiction* 34 (Fall 1992): 49–62.

Wymard, Eleanor B. "A New Version of the Midas Touch: *Daniel Martin* and *The World According to Garp*." *Modern Fiction Studies* 27 (Summer 1981): 284–86.

Acknowledgments

"Garp: Death in the Family" by Greil Marcus from *Rolling Stone* (published in two parts, 24 August 1978 and 21 September 1978). © 1978 by Greil Marcus. Reprinted with permission.

"Domesticated Madness" by Benjamin DeMott from *Atlantic Monthly* 248, no. 4 (October 1981). © 1981 by the Atlantic Monthly Company. Reprinted with permission.

"Structure in the Worlds of John Irving" by Michael Priestly from *Critique: Studies in Modern Fiction* 23, no. 1 (1981). © 1981 by the Helen Dwight Reid Educational Foundation. Reprinted with permission.

"Reservations" by Robert Towers from *The New York Review of Books* 28, no. 17 (5 November 1981). © 1981 by NYREV, Inc. Reprinted with permission.

"Why Is John Irving So Popular?" by Joseph Epstein from *Commentary* 73, no. 6 (June 1982). © 1982 by the American Jewish Committee. Reprinted with permission.

"The Good Wrestler" by Gabriel Miller from *John Irving*. © 1982 by Frederick Ungar Publishing Co. Reprinted with permission.

"John Irving's Aesthetics of Accessibility" (originally titled "John Irving's Aesthetics of Accessibility: Setting Free the Novel") by Jane Bowers Hill from *South Carolina Review* 16, no. 1 (Fall 1983). © 1983 by Clemson University. Reprinted with permission.

"The Postmodern Novel: The Example of John Irving's *The World According to Garp*" by Raymond J. Wilson III from *Critique: Studies in Modern Fiction* 34, no. 1 (Fall 1992). © 1992 by the Helen Dwight Reid Educational Foundation. Reprinted with permission.

"The Family Romances of John Irving" by Debra Shostak from *Essays in Literature* 21, no. 1 (Spring 1994). © 1994 by Western Illinois University. Reprinted with permission.

"Hero Worship and Hermeneutic Dialectics: John Irving's *A Prayer for Owen Meany*" by Philip Page from *Mosaic* 28 (September 1995). © 1995 by *Mosaic*. Reprinted with permission.

"Saints, Sinners and the Dickensian Novel: The Ethics of Storytelling in John Irving's *The Cider House Rules*" by Todd F. Davis and Kenneth Womack from *Style: Family Systems Psychotherapy and Literature/Literary Criticism* 32, no. 2 (August 1998). © 1998 by *Style*. Reprinted with permission.

Index